T0247615

HOW TO
DAO

HOW TO
DAO

Mastering the Future of
Internet Coordination

OWOCKI
and
PUNCAR

PORTFOLIO | PENGUIN

Portfolio / Penguin
An imprint of Penguin Random House LLC
penguinrandomhouse.com

Most Portfolio books are available at a discount when purchased in quantity for sales promotions
or corporate use. Special editions, which include personalized covers, excerpts, and corporate
imprints, can be created when purchased in large quantities. For more information, please call
(212) 572-2232 or e-mail specialmarkets@penguinrandomhouse.com. Your local bookstore can
also assist with discounted bulk purchases using the Penguin Random House corporate
Business-to-Business program. For assistance in locating a participating retailer,
e-mail B2B@penguinrandomhouse.com.

Book design by Nicole LaRoche

LIBRARY OF CONGRESS CATALOGING-IN-PUBLICATION DATA
Names: Owocki, Kevin, author. | Puncar, author.
Title: How to DAO : mastering the future of internet coordination /
Kevin Owocki and Puncar.
Description: New York : Portfolio/Penguin, [2025]
Identifiers: LCCN 2024022673 (print) | LCCN 2024022674 (ebook) |
ISBN 9780593713778 (hardcover) | ISBN 9780593713785 (ebook)
Subjects: LCSH: Finance—Technological innovations.
Classification: LCC HG173 .O96 2025 (print) | LCC HG173 (ebook) |
DDC 332—dc23/eng/20240614
LC record available at https://lccn.loc.gov/2024022673
LC ebook record available at https://lccn.loc.gov/2024022674

Printed in the United States of America
1st Printing

For my parents. Do you understand what I do now, Mom?

For generation alpha. May you inherit a world better than the one your grandparents did.

—OWOCKI

For my family. I am very proud of the business you have built and what you have taught me. I am writing this to enable more small businesses to thrive in any part of the world.

For all leaders. Empowering people around you creates more value than harnessing it for yourself.

—PUNCAR

Contents

FOREWORD   xi

INTRODUCTION   xv

Part One
DAOs 101

1 | What Is a DAO?   3

2 | Why Crypto?   11

3 | How Was the First DAO Created?   19

4 | Why DAOs?   27

Part Two
Exploring the World of DAOs

5 | How to Join a DAO   41

6 | How to Use DAOs to Create Impact   57

7 | How to Use DAOs to Get Paid   73

8 | How to Use Decentralized Finance   95

9 | How to Invest with DAOs   111

10 | How to Use DAOs to Join Social Clubs   123

Part Three

Achieving DAO Mastery

11 | Why (and How) Gitcoin Became a DAO   135

12 | Why Start a DAO?   151

13 | How to Build a DAO   161

Part Four

The Future of DAOs

14 | How to Evolve Decentralized Entities   181

15 | How to Legally Protect Yourself in DAO-Land   197

16 | How to Explore the Frontier of DAOs   207

17 | How DAOs Could Reshape the World   217

Conclusion   235

APPENDIX   239

    A History of DAOs: A Time Line   239

    Key Terms   241

ACKNOWLEDGMENTS   247

Foreword

DON TAPSCOTT

This book explores nothing less than the biggest challenge to the corporation in a century.

Throughout capitalism's history, the corporation has been the foundation of production, wealth creation, and prosperity. The newest titans of the digital age have booted up a new model, the decentralized autonomous organization (DAO), which I believe will shake the foundations of every industry and economy—for the better.

In 1995, I wrote *The Digital Economy: Promise and Peril in the Age of Networked Intelligence.* The internet and World Wide Web had just emerged commercially, and everyone was figuring out how it would change business. I cited Nobel Prize–winning economist Ronald Coase, who, in his 1937 paper, "The Nature of the Firm," asked why corporations exist.

His answer? "Transaction costs," namely the costs of searching for, contracting, and coordinating production factors. These costs were more expensive in an open market than inside a firm. He posited that a firm would expand until the cost of performing a transaction inside exceeded the cost outside. Consequently, twentieth-century capitalists vertically integrated their firms across the value chain.

In *The Digital Economy*, I argued that the internet would reduce transaction costs and lead to more networked business models, which it did, somewhat. Search engines reduced search costs. Applications like email, social media, enterprise resource planning, and cloud computing reduced coordination costs. Firms began to outsource, crowdsource innovation, and eliminate intermediaries, freeing industries to consolidate assets and operations.

However, the internet's impact on corporate architecture has been peripheral. The industrial-age hierarchy remains capitalism's foundation, partly because the internet also dropped transaction costs inside firms. Executives still consider this a better model for managing intangible assets like talent, brands, intellectual property, knowledge, and culture.

Also, the internet hasn't dropped what financial economists Michael Jensen and William Meckling called "agency costs"—the costs of ensuring everyone inside the firm acts in the owner's interest. Nobel Prize–winning economist Joseph Stiglitz argued that firms' size and complexity have increased agency costs even as transaction costs plummeted—hence the huge pay gap between CEOs and frontline employees. This concentration of power and wealth has worsened economic and social inequities.

This dynamic began to shift with blockchain's increasing use. In our 2016 book, *Blockchain Revolution*, Alex Tapscott and I argued that this new "internet of value" could diminish transaction costs in an open market and eliminate many agency costs. The result would be radically new models of orchestrating resources in our economy and society. Networks could do what corporations once did, often better, in a distributed rather than concentrated way.

That's happening today, with the DAO, user-owned and governed networks that can steward huge resources and create value in the economy, as the most important new entity. Visionary leaders can now launch truly decentralized organizations, based on powerful networks owned by their participants and acting autonomously in their own self-interest.

Smart contracts—blockchain-based software that automates many search, contracting, and coordination activities—encode, monitor, and self-police agreements between people and organizations. They can automatically execute payments as conditions are met.

Digital tokens, which are value containers, allow contributors to participate in decision-making and receive compensation for the value they create. In DAOs running on public blockchains, transactions are transparent, reducing many transaction costs and building trust among token holders and the public. Our work at the Blockchain Research Institute provides strong evidence that DAOs are not just better vehicles for innovation, coordination, collaboration, and wealth creation but can also help make the global economy fairer, more inclusive, and more democratic.

The implications of DAOs are staggering. Agency costs are reduced because DAO participants are also economic stakeholders. DAOs are challenging entire industries. Now software can do what most banks do. This isn't fintech, which is simply a new coat of paint on a legacy industry's ancient walls. It's an entirely new industry called decentralized finance or DeFi.

. Scientific inquiry is another area of impact. Decentralized science (DeSci) is a new DAO-based approach to power human effort in fields from medical devices and pharmaceuticals to artificial intelligence and climate science. DePin refers to decentralized physical infrastructure networks that incentivize many different owners of physical or digital resources like computing power and storage into a user-owned network that can harness more capability than their centralized counterparts. The list goes on.

Management science and our best practices for governing and managing today assume the traditional concept of the firm. How many leading thinkers are aware that management as we know it is about to change? How can a DAO adopt an effective strategy without a top decision-maker? How do people or AI agents plan projects? What are the new rules for engaging talent? How do DAOs get users to participate in governance so that they don't just get captured by their biggest and most vocal stakeholders? Can we create a workable policy framework that allows DAOs to thrive? What happens to the four Rs of the industrial-age human resources department—recruit, retrain, retain, and reward—in a decentralized firm? How does governance work when big decisions are traditionally made by boards of directors?

Exploring these questions motivates this book, *How to DAO*. This practical handbook to the new model of value creation is packed with good examples and sensible advice on creating a DAO, making it work, benefiting from it, and keeping yourself and colleagues out of trouble. As such, it is one of the early important contributions to re-thinking business strategy and management science.

Read on, buckle up, and prosper.

Don Tapscott, CM, is (with Alex Tapscott) the coauthor of the global bestseller *Blockchain Revolution* and cofounder of the Blockchain Research Institute, which advises business and government leaders in many countries. The author of eighteen widely read books about the digital age, Tapscott is an adjunct professor at INSEAD and a chancellor emeritus at Trent University. His (second) TED Talk on blockchain has 7.5 million views on TED.com alone.

Introduction

Have you ever wondered why bureaucrats have the power to print money at will, potentially eroding your savings? Or how New York–based private-equity investors can monopolize critical infrastructure, siphoning resources from the communities they're meant to serve? Why is it that social networks can deplatform us, or steal our data to sell to advertisers, without any due process or compensation? What would be possible if we could build digital community–owned goods and services? Much like a fish oblivious to the water it inhabits, you've likely never truly contemplated the traditional financial system in which we live and operate. It appears to be a constant and "normal" state of being.

In this book we urge you to challenge this assumption, scrutinize the environment you're immersed in, and confront what is "normal." The legacy financial realm has been captured by powerful actors. Crypto shows us an alternative path. In many ways, crypto represents the next Occupy Wall Street movement: an opportunity to go bankless. But now the movement has matured and become more sophisticated. And now it has the tools to effectively coordinate.

How does this movement organize? Through decentralized autonomous organizations, more commonly known as DAOs. There are many types of DAOs: investment DAOs, social DAOs, service DAOs, impact DAOs—just to name a few. Some feel like charitable organizations, some like social clubs; some feel like a workplace, while some resemble more of a dispersed network than a cohesive organization. Others feel more like a religion. Some have failed, and some have massively succeeded. There are DAOs that move millions of dollars every month, and there are DAOs that are ghost towns—the people have all left, but the code continues to run.

While there are many flavors of DAOs, the one thing they all have in common is the ability to share assets, share power, and share cryptographically verifiable truth with anyone who has an internet connection.

Just as the types of DAOs vary widely, so do the motivations to join a DAO. You might join a DAO to make friends. Maybe you want to make some extra money. Maybe you just want to learn the tech. Maybe you are thinking of launching a start-up. Maybe you're tired of the old way of doing things and want to find new opportunities in a new world. Maybe you have found a novel purpose from online friendships or communities, and DAOs are your vehicle for changing the world for the better. Maybe you just want to experience a new vibe.

This book is your no-hype resource to learn the ins and outs of the crypto ecosystem and DAOs. Think of it as your ticket to a seat on the westward train to a new, undiscovered frontier. So make yourself comfortable, and take in the sights. Please be responsible, please be careful, and—always—please remember to have fun.

We hope you enjoy your journey as much as we did.

How We Got Here

KEVIN

Growing up in the suburbs of Philadelphia in the late 1990s, I always liked programming. I tried a handful of experiments, from running AllAdvantage ads to starting a web-hosting company in high school. But as the industry matured, I started down what looked like a more conventional path—I got a computer science degree from the University of Delaware in 2006 and entered the corporate world, working for a mutual fund company.

I soon discovered that the corporate world wasn't for me, and I decided that I wanted to enter the start-up world. Then I picked up a copy of Tim Ferriss's *The 4-Hour Workweek*. Ferriss's book was the lightbulb moment I was looking for, the permission slip I needed to try something new and unconventional. After a string of ~~failures~~ learning experiences, I struck gold. I started building Facebook applications on the social network's newly launched developer platform; one of them, a Flash version of beer pong, went viral. After this experience, I was sure I wanted to try something less conventional. And I knew I wanted to do it while I was young. I applied for a job as chief technology officer with a start-up called Ignighter, and when I received an offer, I had found my golden ticket. At the age of twenty-four, I was able to quit my job. I broke the lease on my apartment and moved to the mountains to become a start-up entrepreneur.

Over the coming years, I gained my entrepreneurial starter kit as well as valuable engineering leadership experience. I also became very active in the local technology community in Boulder, Colorado, where I picked up an ethos called #GiveFirst. In the start-up world,

#GiveFirst means simply trying to help anyone, especially entrepreneurs, without any expectation of getting anything back. By 2017, this #GiveFirst ethos had come to shape my digital-community organizing and engineering work, and I began to wonder whether there was a way to build a platform using open-source software for people to find open-source software developers.

The result was Gitcoin—a double-sided marketplace where engineers could find work and "get coin." If I was lucky (and good enough), maybe Gitcoin could eventually become important to thousands of digital professionals. We could cut out the recruiter middlemen. We'd take what I'd been doing in the Boulder community—creating space for people to build relationships, learn, and get new opportunities—and start to do it widely across the internet.

I built Gitcoin on the Ethereum network—an open-source, decentralized software platform that operates a bit like a digital marketplace, offering hosting services and app deployment without any control from a central authority. It also has its own cryptocurrency, known as Ether. In the old financial system, money for IT would go to some back office on Wall Street. In Ethereum, we could route it through Gitcoin, and it was fertile ground for experimentation.

At first, Gitcoin's core product was known as "bounties." If a developer writes x, she will get y amount of coins. Then, during the 2019–2020 crypto bear market, we pivoted to a hackathon-centered model. But all the while, I was thinking further ahead: How could we truly change the way things are done? One of the products that seemed to have promise was Gitcoin Grants: a Web3 crowdfunding tool that was kind of like a crypto-enabled version of Kickstarter. Instead of saying "if you do x, I will give you y" as the core mechanic behind the bounty's product, Gitcoin Grants essentially enabled those who were already doing y to raise x money for it. It was a little less transactional, a lot more community driven, and, it would turn out, massively more successful.

At the time, a #GiveFirst ethos didn't exist in Web3. Crypto was seeing a period of high growth and over-financialization; it was full of zero-sum games, where for one person to win, another needed to lose. I wanted Gitcoin Grants to be an empirical counterexample that we could all point to and say, "Hey, wait, you can play positive-sum games onchain, and we can all benefit." If the crypto landscape was a dark forest, we could build a Hogwarts where magic can happen and where we could kick off a new more regenerative movement.

But then a new challenge loomed: ensuring fairness and neutrality. Our mission was to help communities fund what matters to them, but it didn't sit right with me that we could—even theoretically—decide who got funded. Or that whoever replaced me as CEO of Gitcoin Holdings one day could decide unilaterally to start extracting from the community. It felt like decentralization could be the answer, and the emerging DAO space seemed to offer solutions to our centralization dilemma. Drawing from my community-management days in Boulder, I was fascinated by the idea of a self-organized community—but on a colossal, internet-native scale. So, after several brainstorming sessions, we explored the transition of Gitcoin Grants from a centralized entity to a DAO. The goal? To empower the community, decentralize product decision-making, kick-start innovation, and truly embody the spirit of giving.

The concept of DAO seemed a perfect fit for Gitcoin's aspirations, offering democratic decision-making environments, resilience against powerful attacks, and predictable, neutral operations. After long hours of research and discussion, the decision was made in December 2020 that Gitcoin needed to become a DAO.

The transformation of Gitcoin from a centralized entity to a DAO was no small feat. Unlike traditional corporations, where hierarchical structures dictate decision-making, the transition aimed to place the power of governance squarely in the hands of its members. Launching Gitcoin's next era of governance was the next logical step, ensuring that the community could genuinely shape Gitcoin's direction. We began to move our services onto a blockchain controlled by this same community, ensuring transparency and true decentralization.

Gitcoin DAO launched on May 25, 2021. This was the beginning of our journey of progressive decentralization. But it was a long road ahead, and we couldn't do it all overnight. We'd need the community to rewrite the stack's legal, governance, product, finance, and technology layers over the coming years. And they did. Looking back, this metamorphosis from Web2 paradigms to this new decentralized ethos was perhaps one of my proudest achievements. And while today I might not sit as Gitcoin's CEO, I've decentralized my power but also my stress. My role as a contributor fills me with pride, and it is nice to bat around ideas with other community members on a public forum, gov.gitcoin.co.

Now I'd really like to pay it forward to you. One of my goals for this book (and its companion digital experience at howtodao.xyz) is to open the door to the better parts of the crypto world to you. Together, we'll learn the skills necessary to thrive in DAOs. Puncar and I will give you the starter kit. And we'll walk the rest of the path together.

PUNCAR

I grew up in a small town called Domažlice in the Czech Republic. My parents were entrepreneurs, and I was four years old when they first got into the hospitality business—starting a restaurant and later a café. Like a lot of small-business owners, my parents spent 150 percent of their time at work, which forced me to become more independent. When I was a little older, while all the other kids went home to watch TV after school, I would help out in the restaurant. Unlike a corporate job, everyone working for the family business seemed more connected to it. It wasn't just about getting a paycheck at the end of the month, and if someone wasn't pulling their weight, it immediately impacted everyone else. It was like a large family working toward a common goal. My father wasn't just running a business; he was passionate about what he wanted to achieve. He insisted on quality and that every customer needed to be satisfied. He was determined to bring better food, coffee, and wine to Domažlice so everyone could taste a piece of Italy. That was his goal: not to be a millionaire but to bring Italy to Domažlice. I went off to university on the other side of the country, and it was hard for me to remain physically involved with the family business. Instead, I thought I'd leverage what I was learning at college in order to support Dad remotely. I wanted to help the little family business innovate and embrace e-commerce, so I built a website and online shop and began expanding the operation into a wholesale business. We "open-sourced" our business model so that other coffee shops could recreate our success story in their own city, and many customers did. It wasn't like a franchise where you need to pay for the brand; it was more like sharing a working model in order to help other entrepreneurs succeed.

But I also wanted to explore the corporate world, so after I finished my master's degree, I landed a job in Prague with Ernst & Young, a huge multinational company that straddled accountancy, HR, tech, and financial-services consulting. I worked in the financial-services department as a UX designer and product manager, helping banks launch online platforms. At that time, in 2017, something interesting was happening in the cryptocurrency space. There was a considerable amount of hype and speculation around what were known as initial coin offerings (ICOs), a type of fundraising mechanism in which a company or organization issues a new cryptocurrency to the public in exchange for funds. That year saw a significant increase in the number of companies and projects launching ICOs, as well as the sheer amount of funds raised through these offerings. Many were launched by start-ups looking to raise capital for their projects, but there were also a number of established companies and organizations entering the space, such as IBM, Microsoft, and JP Morgan, with many projects raising millions of dollars in just a matter of hours or days. The banks I was dealing with wanted to know whether they should be getting involved, and it was my job to educate them. Maybe the time isn't right now, I told them, but it will be in the future. The systems they were using needed to evolve to work in this brave new world. There needed to be proof of concept.

I knew I had more to contribute to EY's blockchain team on a global level, and by chance the company needed someone to work on product development and risk management from its offices in New York City. My then-girlfriend lived there at the time, and so it felt like the stars had aligned. I packed my bags and moved from the Czech Republic to the United States, where I worked on blockchain for one of the largest financial-services companies in the world for the next three years. It was a great job, but I longed to get back into the kind of entrepreneurship I'd grown up with. It was in those small businesses and start-ups where the most innovation was happening, where new ideas formed, where everyone was committed and engaged.

Soon, I discovered my path back to innovation and community: DAOs.

The first DAO I joined was BanklessDAO, dedicated to enabling a world with less reliance on banks and the extractive forces that drive them. Within the DAO, we created Bankless Consulting, one of the first Web3 consulting firms. Its success has been a testament to the power of collective action, bringing together the most brilliant minds from diverse fields to revolutionize the financial system. However, as with any revolutionary movement, we encountered challenges along the way. Despite experiencing numerous highs, including the successful completion of more than thirty projects, our resilience was tested during the downturn in the Web3 market. The shifting demand and fluctuating opportunities in the ecosystem required us to be adaptable. But our steadfast belief in the core values of Web3 and its promise of a better, more decentralized future kept us going.

Bankless Consulting was not the only project I contributed to. I also joined another DAO, Index Coop, an organization designed to make crypto investing simpler. Index Coop held tokens that belonged to other DAOs, creating a pool of tokens similar to the S&P 500 index. During my eight-month tenure, I experienced a roller coaster of learning and immersion into the intricate world of decentralized governance. It was more than just a job; it was also a foray into a realm where empowering community-driven decision-making was more important than financial gains.

Of course, early in my DAO journey, I encountered Gitcoin. Having been involved in open-source software, I understood how difficult it is to secure funding for such projects, and I was eager to support Gitcoin's vision. I strongly believed in its mission of promoting "public goods" by collectively financing and supporting projects that benefited the wider community, such as open-source software, educational resources, and civic projects.

At last, with this knowledge in hand, I left the corporate world for good and set sail for a new frontier. I didn't really have a plan; I just knew that I wanted to work in this new and vibrant ecosystem of

DAOs. It was a way of revisiting my father's vision of bringing a small piece of Italy to our hometown. I knew it was his heart driving that decision, and the same thing was now happening to me: it was my destiny to work in this ecosystem that resembled community businesses rather than having a corner office in one of the New York highrises. And now I want to share my vision with you.

Part One

DAOs 101

1

WHAT IS A DAO?

et's start with the basics. *DAO* stands for "decentralized autonomous organization." You can think of DAOs as digitally native vehicles for organizing a network of humans toward a common goal. Compared with traditional organizations, they have an internal economic model already built in thanks to blockchain, allowing for smooth financial coordination. DAO membership is collective, with decisions made from the bottom up rather than the top down.

The rules of a DAO are embedded in the code itself on a blockchain— a decentralized, incorruptible digital ledger that securely encrypts data and can execute smart contracts—eliminating the need for a central governing body. A blockchain records transactions across many computers in a way that prevents any future alteration of the record without the consensus of the network. This technology is enabled by a peer-to-peer network, where participants can directly interact without needing trusted intermediaries (such as banks). It provides transparency, security, and immutability without a centralized authority, which is why it's the backbone of crypto assets like BTC and ETH, or DAO assets like GTC. It even has applications beyond financial transactions—for example, Web3 social networks allow users to manage their own identity, instead of being beholden to giant technology companies.

Just like how traditional organizations have a bank account, many

DAOs have a shared treasury. And just like most traditional organizations are incorporated in a legal jurisdiction, DAOs are incorporated onchain. When a dispute arises among members of a traditional organization, it is settled in court. When a dispute arises among members of a DAO, it is settled onchain.

In their most simple form, DAOs can be thought of as a "group chat with a bank account." This is a phrase coined by investor Cooper Turley, and because of its simplicity, it has since gone viral.

Many DAOs have "one commandment": something they believe is wrong with the world that they aim to change by rallying people from around the globe. This is usually a meme or a phrase that can be concisely stated and shared by its members. For example, Gitcoin wants to "fund what matters," creating a space for people who believe in backing causes that enhance the world, even if there is no direct financial benefit to them. Similarly, MakerDAO is on a mission to construct the first unbiased currency, appealing to those who feel that the current financial system is unfair and wish to reform it.

Yet it's crucial to recognize that DAOs are not only about addressing what's wrong or deficient but are equally about pioneering something fresh and innovative. They leverage the borderless nature of digital coordination, assembling a diverse group of people across the world to not only facilitate change but also to give birth to new, vibrant initiatives and entities that reflect their collective ideas and skills. This union of alteration and creation is central to a DAO, enabling it to navigate uncharted territories and conceive radical possibilities in a decentralized, internet-native world. Not only can they be accessed from anywhere like traditional websites, they also can be governed from anywhere, meaning that someone across the world can be your partner in your DAO, putting everyone on the same footing.

Are DAOs companies? Sometimes, but not always. In its purest form, a DAO has no centralized governing body, and decisions flow bottom up through proposals on a public forum. Rules are enforced by code, and there are no executive roles. Don't be fooled by the word *organization*. As opposed to hierarchical organizations, DAOs can resemble networks of individuals more than traditional organizations.

The aperture of the DAO world is very wide, which can present challenges in reasoning about them in the abstract. To ground our discussion in the tangible, we will get into examples later in the book. To begin, just know that DAOs encompass a range of utilities. Some DAOs exist to distribute money; others are designed to make investments. Some exist to facilitate social connections among members, others to collect digital artifacts like NFTs.

DAOs are really good at:

- Providing equal access for everybody, from anywhere.
- Providing a way to earn from anywhere.
- Providing tools for making better democratic decisions.
- Providing tools to evade censorship or attacks from powerful entities.
- Providing tools to create credible fairness, where traits like predictability, adaptability, and neutrality are valued above efficiency.
- Providing tools to establish internal economic (tokenomic) systems that incentivize and coordinate members toward a common mission.
- Providing tools to coordinate without relying on an intermediary between you and your transactions.
- Providing audit trails.
- Confusing your older relatives about what it is that you do for work.

DAOs are a new frontier in human coordination. At a time in which our Industrial Age institutions are lumbering, creaking, and failing to capture the support of the populations they serve, DAOs offer a new way to create Information Age institutions that can be democratically governed by the very populations they serve.

The DAO ecosystem is in a constant state of evolution. Every new experiment leads to new lessons that can accelerate the next experiment. There will be giant successes in the future and giant failures. In many ways we are just at the beginning of the journey.

CHAPTER SUMMARY:
What Is a DAO?

- **DECENTRALIZED COLLABORATION:** DAOs break down geographical and hierarchical boundaries, enabling global, seamless collaboration without central control.

- **AUTONOMY AND SELF-EXECUTION:** Through smart contracts, DAOs autonomously execute decisions, manage resources, and uphold rules, diminishing the need for intermediaries.

- **NURTURING INNOVATION:** DAOs are a hub for global transformative initiatives, leveraging collective ideas and talents to drive creative innovation.

2

WHY CRYPTO?

I n order to understand DAOs, you must understand the environment in which they've sprouted: the crypto ecosystem.

The beginning of the modern crypto movement began with Satoshi Nakamoto, the pseudonymous person or group of people who created Bitcoin, the first and most well-known cryptocurrency. The true identity of Satoshi Nakamoto is unknown, and it remains one of the greatest mysteries in the tech world. In 2008, Nakamoto published a paper outlining his ideas for a new digital currency and, in 2009, he released the first Bitcoin software, which launched the network and the first units of this new cryptocurrency, which Nakamoto called Bitcoins.

The primary invention behind crypto is Satoshi's solution to what's known as the Byzantine Generals' Problem. This is a term originating from a thought experiment in computer science, particularly in the field of distributed computing (connecting several computers to solve one problem in tandem) and decentralized systems. It highlights the difficulties that several parties can encounter when trying to agree on a single course of action in an unreliable communication substrate (like the internet), symbolized by the challenge faced by a group of generals who are trying to coordinate an attack while situated in different locations.

Satoshi solved this problem within the context of digital currency by implementing blockchain technology in Bitcoin. Transactions are verified and agreed upon on a public ledger without requiring trust in a central authority. Through a process called mining, the people functioning as network participants (also called miners) solve complex mathematical puzzles to "seal" each block of transactions and link them in a chain. This system makes it extremely difficult for a bad actor to change the historical record or introduce fraudulent transactions, for they would need to command a majority of the system's computational power (a situation commonly referred to as a "51 percent attack").

This innovation was extended in 2013 with the Ethereum white paper. Vitalik Buterin, the cofounder of Ethereum, did not directly extend Bitcoin's functionality; instead, he created a completely new platform, Ethereum, which has some similarities to Bitcoin but is fundamentally different in terms of capabilities and purpose. Ethereum enables "smart contracts," self-executing contracts where the terms are directly written into code and automatically enacted. These contracts run on the Ethereum blockchain, making them tamperproof and independent of any central authority, and they can handle a broad range of applications beyond simple monetary transactions. For the first time, anyone could create and program their values into money. This created a massive new design space, and it had profound implications for what types of economies could be built in the coming decades.

One of the things smart contracts enabled was the creation of DAOs. Now you could incorporate an organization onchain using a smart contract and facilitate the creation of a new internet-native coordination mechanism.

A significant early figure associated with the formalization and promotion of DAOs as we understand them today is Daniel Larimer.

He is known for creating the concept of a decentralized autonomous corporation (DAC), which can be considered an early form of a DAO. He discussed these ideas in 2013 and 2014 in the context of the Bit-Shares project, a decentralized platform that he cofounded. These concepts were part of broader discussions within the community about decentralized governance.

Buterin played a crucial role in popularizing the concept of DAOs. He believed that decentralized governance could enhance the capital-allocation process and optimize the investment and use of a company's resources. In this model, organizations decentralize themselves to build trust among the participants, thereby excluding groups that fail to do this from the economic benefits of the "circle of trust."

The term *DAO* became significantly more well-known following "The DAO" project launch on the Ethereum platform in 2016. This DAO was a specific organization, but its publicity brought considerable attention to the idea of decentralized autonomous organizations as a whole.

Despite this publicity, and growing public awareness, confusion around DAOs persists, and it is our belief that DAOs cannot be understood in words only. You need to experience them to understand them, and the knowledge in this book is designed to pair with hands-on knowledge gained by playing with crypto. Keep an eye out as you browse through the book for boxes with Quests in them. Inside each Quest box is a practical thing you can do in crypto. For more comprehensive instructions and practical exercises, please visit our website, howtodao.xyz/quest.

QUEST 1: Get a wallet.

If you're new to the world of crypto, the first step is to acquire a wallet, which will enable you to begin engaging with different decentralized applications.

Here is our first quest: Set up your Ethereum wallet and sign in with it to our website.

Metamask and Coinbase Wallet are the two most popular wallets. On their official websites, you can find detailed instructions on how to install them on your phone or computer.

Once you've completed the installation, head over to howtodao.xyz and click on the sign-up option. Choose the wallet option and use your newly created wallet to connect. Congratulations, you are now a true Web3 user!

As a Web3 user, be cautious when installing your new wallet or interacting with other sites. Always make sure to only use the official website to avoid falling for phishing attempts.

You can find detailed instructions at howtodao.xyz/quest.

CHAPTER SUMMARY:
Why Crypto?

- **BITCOIN'S EMERGENCE:** Introduced by the pseudonymous entity Satoshi Nakamoto in 2008, Bitcoin pioneered the use of blockchain technology, allowing for decentralized, peer-to-peer transfer of digital value without a central authority. It laid the groundwork for the development of subsequent cryptocurrencies and related technologies.

- **ETHEREUM'S DEVELOPMENT:** Vitalik Buterin launched Ethereum in 2015, building on Bitcoin's foundational blockchain technology but introducing smart contracts and the Ethereum Virtual Machine (EVM). This platform's capabilities allowed for more complex financial operations, decentralized applications (DApps), and the facilitation of initial coin offerings (ICOs), significantly expanding the blockchain's use cases beyond mere currency.

- **THE RISE OF DAOS:** The concept of decentralized autonomous organizations (DAOs) evolved, influenced by early cypherpunk ideas and discussions within the cryptocurrency community. The launch of "The DAO" in 2016, a complex set of smart contracts running on Ethereum, marked a significant turn in understanding the potentials and risks of fully decentralized, autonomous organizational structures and governance.

3

HOW WAS THE FIRST DAO CREATED?

n the spring of 2016, the world of cryptocurrency was rocked by an event that would come to be known as The DAO hack. The downfall of what was one of the first DAOs would ultimately help identify flaws and ensure that the entire concept of DAOs could survive into the future. Confusingly, it centered around an organization simply known as The DAO, which we briefly introduced in the previous chapter. Nowadays there are dozens of DAOs, but back then "The DAO" was really the only DAO out there.

The story begins in November 2015, when Slock.it, an ambitious project that was kind of like "Craigslist-meets-AI-meets-Ethereum," launched the world's first decentralized investment fund, allowing the company to seek funding through smart contracts encoded on the blockchain. The fund was known as The DAO, and it launched in April 2016. Interested investors could exchange Ether (the native cryptocurrency of Ethereum) for DAO tokens—tokens being a unit of ownership that represents your rights to something—enabling them to vote on projects and start-ups to get funded. Successful applicants would receive funding from The DAO treasury, and if their projects were profitable, investors would also benefit from the upside. This was a new type of investment vehicle: essentially a decentralized venture-capital fund, an experiment in crowdfunding built on the Ethereum blockchain that allowed anyone to invest in a pool of money that would be used to back various projects, all without the need for intermediaries like banks or brokers.

By the end of Slock.it's twenty-eight-day crowdfunding round, The DAO held a phenomenal $150 million worth of Ether from more than eleven thousand investors—14 percent, in fact, of all the Ether in circulation. The DAO was one of the largest crowdfunding campaigns in history, and as a result, The DAO was hailed as a groundbreaking innovation in the world of finance. But it was not without its flaws. It had not been subject to the same rigorous security audits, and this weakness would ultimately prove to be its downfall. In the early hours of June 17, 2016, an unknown attacker began siphoning funds from the business because of a vulnerability in the smart-contract code that governed its operations. The attack went unnoticed at first, but as more and more funds were drained from the organization, panic began to set in. The DAO's administrators scrambled to find a way to stop the attack, but not before $50 million worth of crypto had been stolen.

As the news of The DAO hack spread, it sent shock waves through the world of crypto. Many began to question the viability of the entire blockchain ecosystem, and some predicted that the hack would be the death knell for Ethereum, the platform on which The DAO was built. But The DAO hack was not the result of a flaw in the blockchain technology, and the Ethereum community refused to concede defeat. Within days of the attack, a group of developers proposed a radical solution: to "fork" the Ethereum blockchain—essentially creating two different versions, each with its own set of transaction records and history—and create a new version that would erase the effects of The DAO hack. Ultimately, the decision to create a new version of Ethereum was adopted by a majority of Ethereum operators. The result meant there were now two separate versions of the network: the original chain, which became known as Ethereum Classic. (Ethereum Classic wanted to keep everything as is because it followed a philosophy known as Code Is Law: if the code has a bug that has been exploited, we should just accept that outcome and learn from it.) The new chain was simply called Ethereum. For the new version, the hard fork effectively reversed the hack, restoring the stolen funds to its owners.

In the end, The DAO hack proved to be a turning point for the cryptocurrency world. It exposed the vulnerabilities of even the most cutting-edge blockchain technologies, but it also demonstrated the resilience and adaptability of the community that had built them. The Ethereum hard fork was a controversial move, but it showed that the decentralized nature of blockchain technology made it possible for users to collectively take control of their own financial destinies. In a way, The DAO hack needed to happen. All failures have consequences, but they may also open new opportunities. The crypto ecosystem is full of thousands of experiments blossoming, together speed-running the history of finance. Some go extinct; others rise from the ashes and fill the evolutionary niche of their fallen predecessors. The DAO hack has informed the design of many DAOs since then.

But DAOs showed such promise that the collapse of The DAO just couldn't bury this revolutionary concept forever. DAOs had the potential to change the way we think about organizations for the better, enabling a more democratic, inclusive, and transparent way of doing business, as well as addressing some of the most pressing challenges facing traditional organizations today and reducing the risk of corruption, collusion, and abuse of power.

Although a DAO nuclear winter followed the implosion of The DAO in 2016, a new DAO arose just a few years later, in 2019, that helped get the movement back on track: MolochDAO. MolochDAO was the first sprout of spring for DAOs. It learned from The DAO hack and built a simplified DAO framework that is incredibly difficult, perhaps impossible, to exploit. We'll go further into what MolochDAO actually does later in the book, but it's important to understand now that MolochDAO proved that DAOs could be secure and stable ecosystems, restoring trust and offering a path forward—one that allowed for all the positives that made people so excited about The DAO in the first place: reducing corruption, ensuring more ethical and sustainable business practices, and facilitating decision-making for the benefit of all stakeholders, rather than just a select few.

The DAO hack incentivized developers to develop DAO standards that were simple, well audited, and tested, in order to keep funds safe. Once MolochDAO offered a new proof of concept, then new DAOs sprang up in its place, many of which are surviving and thriving to this day.

QUEST 2: Send crypto to your wallet.

Web2 giants like Facebook and Google are able to provide free service only because they sell your data to marketers. The Web3 movement empowers users to take ownership of their data and identities, but in exchange it requires users to pay small fees in order to free the ecosystem from these exploitative Web2 practices.

To really explore the world of DAOs and Web3, it's worth investing in a little bit of ETH, which you can then use to buy into any number of other marketplaces and navigate freely. Think of it like visiting another country: of course, you're going to need to get some of the local currency in order to participate.

Connect to your centralized exchange, such as Coinbase, Binance, or OKX, and send a fraction of ETH from there to your wallet address.

As always, you can find detailed instructions at howtodao.xyz/quest.

CHAPTER SUMMARY:
A Brief History of the First DAO

- The first DAO, known simply as The DAO, became one of the most successful crowdfunding campaigns in history, raising $150 million in Ether and proving the viability of DAOs.

- However, a technological vulnerability enabled a hacker to siphon off $50 million worth of crypto, leading to questions about the viability of the whole enterprise.

- In response to the hack, the Ethereum community decided to fork the technology. The result meant there were now two separate versions of the network: the original chain, which became known as Ethereum Classic, and the new chain, simply called Ethereum.

4

WHY DAOs?

T here are three ways to understand crypto:

1. Crypto as money
2. Crypto as tech
3. Crypto as coordination

Money's value is underpinned by trust within a society or an economic system. Think of a dollar bill: its value is not inherent but guaranteed by the US government and agreed upon by users. The USD is considered a fiat currency because it is backed by trust in the US government rather than based on a physical commodity like gold or silver. And as we've seen in recent years, USD can be printed according to the whims of the federal bureaucracy.

The appeal of crypto assets like BTC or ETH is that their supply is guaranteed by math and game theory rather than a particular nation-state, providing them with a measure of insulation from political instability and allowing them to be used across borders.

Meanwhile, blockchain technology and traditional banking mainframes operate on fundamentally different architectures and philosophies. Banking mainframes rely on centralized databases, where a single entity, like a bank or a consortium of banks, controls the data and transaction processing. These centralized systems have been the backbone of the financial industry for decades, providing a reliable, secure, and efficient environment for large-scale and high-speed data processing. However, they are susceptible to internal failures, fraud, and cyberattacks because of their reliance on a single point of control.

Comparatively, blockchain offers several paradigm shifts from traditional banking mainframes: improved security through decentralization, transparency with its public ledger system, and potentially reduced costs by eliminating intermediaries. Blockchain technology stores data across a network of computers, creating an immutable public ledger. This decentralization increases trust in the system, making it highly resistant to tampering or alteration by any one party. Transactions on a blockchain are verified by a consensus mechanism among participants in the network, often called nodes, enhancing the integrity of the data recorded.

Crypto fundamentally changes the trust assumptions for individuals working together across the internet. The design space for DAOs—multiple individuals using a crypto network to manage their commitments to one another—is very new. In some ways, DAOs are really a catchall term for many types of organizations that are domiciled on the blockchain, enabling truly global movements.

So how will the DAO world differ from the traditional world with which we are already familiar? The design space for DAOs is vast. We've now got programmable money, so what types of new economic systems could be created? How will human coordination evolve now that we can make easily enforceable commitments to one another? There is no easy way to know exactly how the DAO space will evolve, but there are ways that we can infer how it might grow.

The New World of DAOs versus the Old World of Web2

DAOs stand in stark contrast to the world of Web2, where the landscape is populated by internet giants like Meta and Google. That world, where the tech behemoths are in control and have a fiduciary duty to shareholders to put profits over people, uses your data to monetize you. It also locks you into their ecosystem, preventing you from easily porting your data to rival networks. And they have been plagued by security fears and concerns over the hoarding and trafficking of your personal data. The world where we are all serfs on Zuckerberg's turf, Google's data centers, Bezosland, or Elon's fiefdom? We are leaving that world behind.

Web2 was about information sharing, but Web3 is about value exchange and ownership, and DAOs are a fundamental part of that mission—the evolution of the internet. DAOs are an upgrade to the internet that uses blockchain, cryptocurrencies, and smart contracts to disrupt intermediaries and put control firmly back in the hands of the people. This technology could let people all over the world create this new web together, and key to this is decentralization—hosting platforms and apps on the numerous servers that belong to the people who use them rather than on the server of a huge multinational company with a power-hungry CEO and a board of directors legally bound to maximize company profits, bonuses, and dividends for its shareholders.

Some DAOs may begin to take on functions traditionally associated with nation-states or nongovernmental organizations (NGOs). Ideally, your government uses your tax dollars to fund public goods—

things like roads and bridges—or to fund science and research, all intended to improve the lives of its citizens. But it's not within the purview of actual nation-states to fund digital infrastructure for the world at large. DAOs could be designed to fill this gap. For example, open-source software is a cross-border, global, public good, one that generates almost $400 billion per year in value, and open-source software is the foundation of the DAO ecosystem. Because DAOs can be built on global ledgers, they have the potential to address major coordination failures that impact everyone on the planet. For instance, they could facilitate crowdfunding for open-source software projects, ensuring that initiatives beneficial to all are adequately funded—Gitcoin has already funded tens of millions of dollars' worth of open-source software. Additionally, DAOs could verify that people are fulfilling their commitments by using cryptographic methods to ensure trust and track impact.

Many DAOs work on a more equitable system of compensation. They don't care where you live; everyone is paid according to the same policies. In these DAOs, you're assessed on your skills, not where you live. Whether you're in the United States, the Czech Republic, or Nigeria, DAOs could allow you to generate wealth based on your impact and input. If you're working for a DAO from a country where you can't trust your bank not to seize your money, getting paid in crypto means your finances are more secure. We are creating a new sovereign financial system that cannot be unilaterally shut down by any institution that wishes to sidestep due process. If you're in a part of the world without great financial infrastructure, where your paychecks can take weeks to land in your accounts, you can still get paid on the Ethereum network in fifteen seconds (the time it takes for a block of transactions to be mined). If you're based in a country like Argentina, where in 2022 inflation hit a thirty-year high of 95 percent, and you don't want to see your savings disappear, then there's a huge opportunity for you. Instead of holding the local currency, hold crypto tokens that you can access from anywhere. If you can get paid in ETH, USD, or any other currency that isn't hyperinflationary, that's a pretty big game changer. Or if you want to send money back home to a loved one, instead of using Western Union and paying a 10 percent transfer fee, you can use the blockchain network and pay just a few cents per transfer, with a currency no one can seize. (This becomes even more essential for people in truly life-threatening situations, like refugees or those seeking asylum; rather than carrying physical cash that can be taken from them, they merely need to memorize their passcode and then be able to access their money from anywhere in the world.)

You can even get paid in a US dollar–denominated token known as a stablecoin. So even if you are in a country with an unstable financial system, thanks to the blockchain you can leverage the stability of the world's reserve currency—the US dollar—by accessing stablecoins like $DAI or $USDC.

It's one thing to describe these hypotheticals—it's another to see them in action. That's why it's worth considering the story of Isaac Onuwa, a thirty-two-year-old computer programmer from Ebonyi in southeast Nigeria. Isaac is whip-smart and entrepreneurial, and he worked as a part-time developer in the Gitcoin network from 2018 to 2021. That's how we first heard about Isaac and his remarkable story.

Isaac initiated his Web3 journey by executing bounties on the Gitcoin bounty board for various Web3 projects and also selected a couple of bounties to enhance the Gitcoin protocol itself. That's when Kevin (and other funders in the network) noticed him and his remarkable skills, leading them to start working together on a more regular basis. Whereas a developer working for a Nigerian tech firm might expect to earn an average of 120,000 nairas per month—approximately $260—Isaac, working for DAOs (including Gitcoin and a few others), began earning more than 910,000 nairas per month, or $2,000, multiplying his salary by nearly eight times. Contributors to the DAO were often paid the same rate, based solely on their contributions, not their locations.

Getting paid in crypto meant Isaac had access to his hard-earned money any time he wanted, and from anywhere. In Nigeria it wasn't unheard of for a bank's network to go down or to seize your payment in the middle of a transaction, which meant you couldn't withdraw your cash. It often meant ATMs were down, too. But all Isaac had to do was ask a techie friend if he could trade with them, and they'd give him the cash he needed in return for the equivalent in crypto paid into their secure account. It was so much easier than having to wait until the bank restored the network.

Isaac's story illuminates a broader shift from the old, industrial ways to the new, internet-native age, involving massive changes in how we handle money and work. DAOs and working in cryptocurrency, like Isaac does, represent a bet on updating our financial systems during this shift. Especially as older, post–World War II systems prove less reliable or adaptable, using cryptocurrency is more than a speculative move. It's a practical innovation that safeguards individuals like Isaac from the limitations or breakdowns of traditional banking systems, offering a consistent and global approach to earning and accessing income.

If you are based in the United States, you may remember reading in high school about the pioneers going west along the Oregon Trail in the 1800s, planting their seed in the frontier in order to find adventure, prosperity, and a new life in the future. Many different generations have had their own frontiers. Baby boomers had theirs—they were the hippies who bought houses in the 1970s or 1980s for $20,000 that are now worth a million dollars. The frontier for the baby boom generation was real estate and stocks, and participating in the upside of the growing economy. For our generation, the frontier is technology. And to extend the "Go West" metaphor further, our westward frontier is the frontier of crypto, the digital equivalent of the old pioneer routes where you had to ford the river and avoid a snake bite, but where if you made it, you had the potential to start afresh on new foundations. There is a ton of upside if you're a successful pioneer in this industry. You can go out and stake your own claim of belonging, ownership, and income. That's what's so exciting about it. But it genuinely takes curiosity, vision, grit, dynamism, and skill to forgo a more comfortable and financially rewarding career on autopilot for the uncertainty of the frontier. The frontier is not cushy, it can be risky, and it's not for everyone.

We're still in the early days of DAOs. It'll take time for us to get it right. After all, the old financial system has been evolving for hundreds of years. Crypto is only a decade old, and DAOs are even newer. It'll take a while for the capital flooding in and out of these new businesses—capital that is distributed meritocratically based on novel compensation algorithms—to impact traditional economies in any meaningful way. In the meantime we'll still see crypto millionaires and billionaires. But crypto has the capacity to improve the standard of living and education and health care for those who use it. We can slowly nurture this trend around the world.

QUEST 3: Create an ENS name.

In crypto, wallets don't just hold your financial assets; they also represent your identity in the Web3 space. Everywhere you go, everywhere you log in with your account, your wallet will show up as your ENS name. ENS is the Ethereum name service. It is essentially like a decentralized naming protocol, built on the Ethereum ecosystem. Think of it as a username or a domain name, but for Ethereum.

That's why, before you join a DAO, you need to get yourself an ENS name and create your Web3 identity. Imagine voting in DAOs. When members get distributed tokens in order to vote on proposals, their ENS names will show up with their votes, helping everyone to understand where everyone else stands and getting to know their fellow DAO members. You can register a dot ETH name of five characters or more for $5 a year, for as many years as you like.

To get an ENS name, go to ens.domains and follow the prompts.

As always, you can find detailed instructions at howtodao.xyz/quest.

CHAPTER SUMMARY:

Why DAOs?

Isaac Onuwa's story stands as a testament to the transformative potential of DAOs and cryptocurrency, illuminating a pathway toward an inclusive, decentralized, and equitable future, particularly for individuals in regions where traditional systems have faltered or failed to offer security and opportunities.

- The three lenses for understanding crypto are money, tech, and coordination.

- DAOs are built on blockchains; therefore, they are transparent, global, incorruptible, programmable, and open source.

- DAOs cultivate a borderless collaborative workforce by valuing contributions and erasing socioeconomic barriers.

- Cryptocurrencies promise financial alternatives that support user control, especially in regions with unstable traditional finances.

- DAOs level the playing field in international business and could spearhead solutions to global issues like climate change.

Part Two

Exploring the World of DAOs

5

HOW TO JOIN A DAO

By now, we've spent a fair amount of time hopefully persuading you about the merits of DAOS, and how important they could yet become, but we haven't told you how you can get involved.

Every day, people of all ages are joining DAOs, from young developers who don't want to work a 9-to-5 job like their parents did to middle-aged managers who feel like they've hit a ceiling in their current job and are looking for some excitement elsewhere. It's not just tech people joining DAOs, either. There are artists, activists, creators, bankers, and managers. And there is no one single skill that's needed. DAOs are building new coordination mechanisms to co-own, co-govern, and collaboratively work toward a brighter future. You aren't joining a DAO because you want to be in the tech space; you're joining a DAO because you want to explore outside of what's available in the traditional world, and you want something that will be powered by—and organized by—people peer to peer, rather than in a top-down hierarchy.

DAOs are empowering people to build new stuff, and they are not limited, as corporations are, to maximizing profits and shareholder value. DAOs can be driven by stakeholder governance, not just shareholder governance. And that means much bigger and more important goals, such as fighting climate change or addressing poverty, are possible.

Let's start by taking a look at the DAO landscape as it stands today. Although a DAO can span multiple categories, most can be broadly classified into the following groups:

1. Impact DAOs

An impact DAO coordinates resources to make an impact on society—maybe it's addressing climate change, or perhaps it's designed to come up with a coordinated effort to clean up the ocean or protect forests. Or maybe it's meant to raise money to fund public goods. Impact DAOs, like Gitcoin, are enterprises that coordinate their resources to help fund open-source projects and other public goods, and because there are vast resources of global coordination, they can be far more successful and transparent than traditional approaches. We will look more closely at impact DAOs in Chapter Six.

2. Service and Infrastructure DAOs

Service and infrastructure DAOs essentially assist other DAOs. Their members provide consultancy, maintenance services, or resources, creating a repository of expertise. An example of a service DAO is Bankless Consulting, which presents itself as the world's first Web3-native consulting firm, offering advice to DAOs in the rapidly expanding decentralized economy. Others might provide infrastructure layers, on top of which other Web3 projects can be created or maintained, such as payroll solutions or the creation of DAOs themselves.

3. Social DAOs

Social DAOs are more like clubs. They're designed for groups of people who want to organize around a common topic or theme. An example of a social DAO is FWB, or "Friends with Benefits," a group of Web3-focused thinkers and creators who meet on Discord and in real life to collaborate on projects, events, and products. It calls itself a "decentralized creative studio." New members buy into the DAO so everyone has skin in the game: it has its own cryptocurrency, $FWB, and official FWB members can earn tokens as a reward for participation, as well as collectively decide which projects to fund.

4. Art and Collectibles DAOs

Art and collectibles DAOs are managed by holders of nonfungible tokens (NFTs)—"nonfungible" meaning they're one of a kind, like paintings, rather than exchangeable for each other, like dollar bills—that denote ownership of, for example, a piece of art or music. They exist to provide some kind of coordination mechanism between the creators of that art or music and the owners of the NFTs. Perhaps a singer wants her fans to weigh in on what venue she should play next. Or an artist might ask his collectors to nominate a city for his next gallery show. One example of an art and collectibles DAO is Nouns DAO. It operates like an auction system in which one NFT is sold per day—usually for hundreds of thousands of dollars—and the money from the sale goes into the common treasury. The community of NFT holders decides what to do with the money—like donate some to charity or use it to expand the Nouns brand.

5. Protocol DAOs

A protocol DAO governs specific protocols, meaning the rules by which two or more parties interact. Think about the internet as a protocol. You might be using a Gmail account, and your friend might use Outlook, but you can still send emails to each other because they both run on the same protocol. In the DAO world, protocols encompass the workings of everything from borrowing/lending platforms and decentralized exchanges to other decentralized applications (DApps) and even the underlying blockchain infrastructure itself. Their crucial role ensures the continuous optimization of the rules, operations, and foundational structures of the DAO system. An essential subset of protocol DAOs is that of DeFi DAOs—DAOs dedicated to decentralized finance. These entities play a transformative role in the decentralized financial arena by promoting the development and governance of decentralized financial tools and platforms. One of the most prominent examples of a DeFi DAO is MakerDAO, which operates on the Ethereum blockchain. Its primary role involves the creation and management of a stablecoin called Dai, which is designed to maintain its value in parity with the US dollar.

6. Network States DAOs

Network states DAOs are online communities that can evolve into physical societies. Starting in the internet realm, these communities, empowered by cryptocurrencies and shared values, could transition to tangible spaces, blurring the lines between the digital and physical worlds. Unlike traditional countries, which are bound by geography, these states would arise from shared interests and ideals, offering a modern take on governance and societal organization. Afropolitan, which attempts to create a DAO home for the African diaspora, is one example.

7. Gaming and Virtual Worlds DAOs

Gaming and virtual worlds DAOs are steered by participants who hold in-game assets or tokens that have value within a digital universe. These DAOs are established to facilitate coordination and transactions between in-game stakeholders. Imagine a virtual city where property owners vote on the next architectural design or where gamers decide on the storyline for the next quest. Decentraland is a quintessential example of a virtual world DAO. Users own parcels of digital land in this metaverse, represented as NFTs. Through Decentraland DAO, landowners can influence decisions on software upgrades, in-world policies, or even public-space developments.

You can join a DAO from anywhere—the DAO space is truly global. Traditionally, if you're looking for employment with a US company, you need to be in the United States or have a visa to work there. With DAOs, there are no borders. If you want to contribute and have the right skill set and attitude, you can.

Here are four simple steps to take before joining a DAO. Remember: *Why, What, Who, How?*

1. WHY: Start with learning.

Before you join the Web3 ecosystem, try to understand what it's all about. There is so much information online about Web3 and DAOs, but you can also show up to numerous events in real life. Meet people. Ask questions. And remember: taking baby steps is OK. Crypto is risky, and we should acknowledge that with eyes wide open: you've spent your whole life relying on institutions like banks and governments to protect you, but in order to escape the negative qualities of these things, you need to also take security into your own hands. That means thinking adversarially, doing your own research, and not diving into anything before you have the necessary information.

Go through an OODA loop. OODA stands for:

1. Observe what's around you
2. Orient yourself in what you want to do
3. Decide what to do
4. Act
5. (repeat)

As you ramp up understanding and self-confidence, you can begin to take more assured moves into the DAO space.

2. WHAT: Define your purpose and goals.

What problems is a DAO trying to solve, how is it going to do that, and does that align with your own values? You can join numerous DAOs, and just because you've joined one doesn't mean you can't leave it. Get involved, explore, find your ideal match. Over time, you'll find that some communities are more important to you than others. Don't feel bad about closing a few browser tabs and exiting a few Discord servers along the way.

3. WHO: Join a team or community.

Successful DAOs have strong and engaged communities committed to their vision. Find out what channels they use for members to communicate—perhaps it's Discord, maybe

WhatsApp. Make sure that you read through the guidelines before you join in the discussions. What are the incentives for members? Do contributors benefit financially? Is this even your primary motivation for getting involved? Find out *who* the community is.

4. HOW: Deepen involvement.

Communication and governance are key. How does the DAO coordinate and govern itself? Where are the social spaces for this DAO? Should you become a token holder and get to vote on the most recent DAO proposals?

How you deepen involvement in any specific DAO will depend on that DAO's unique qualities and what types of experiences and opportunities it has to explore.

QUEST 4: Join a DAO's Discord.

Many DAOs coordinate on a chat platform called Discord, which you can download to your computer or mobile device at discord.gg. This is the heart and soul of the DAO, the place where you can really get connected to the community, get to know people, and start to involve yourself with the mission of the DAO. If you really want to advance on your DAO journey, this is the place to do it.

Browse the website of your favorite DAO, where you can find a link to its Discord. Join the Discord of a DAO

> and say "gm" (short for "good morning") in one of the
> channels, and then explore whatever seems interesting
> to you.
>
> As always, you can find detailed instructions at
> howtodao.xyz/quest.

DAOs vary in their onboarding processes. For some, it's very similar to joining a social club or a company; some might be more open and allow you to just enter through the door, whereas others might require you to go through a process. Some DAOs are even old-school enough to make you do a job interview! Many DAOs have active members on social media sites like Twitter, Farcaster, and Lens Protocol—and it never hurts to have a positive social connection before trying to work your way into an organization.

For example, BanklessDAO is open to everyone to come and contribute. You just enter its Discord server and look around to find an interesting project, introducing yourself and asking how you can be helpful. For more information, you can go to howtodao.xyz/banklessDAO.

Meanwhile, working for Gitcoin can mean a few different things. You can submit a GCP—Gitcoin community proposal—on its governance forum and get funding for a project you have designed, kind of like an external service provider. You could fundraise using Gitcoin Grants in the quarterly "citizens rounds"—crowdfunding rounds that support DAO contributors. Or you could go through the more traditional onboarding process by interviewing for a full-time role on one of the DAO workstreams. Before you do either of those things, join the community—that's permissionless, and a lot of fun. Candidates who are proactively involved in the community are often favored in the interview process.

The most important part is to find a DAO you want to contribute to and then follow its process. And to find the right DAO for you, you should do your research. There are no shortcuts. Check what projects there are, what they are doing, and whether a project aligns with your career path and life goals. You can also check job boards for DAO vacancies. We are curating one on our website: howtodao.xyz/jobs.

Remember that courtship is a two-way street. What are your goals? What project resonates with you? What people, what messages? Are the vibes good? Is there anyone trying to scam you? This will be a journey of learning and self-discovery. Be friendly; be courteous; be curious. There are no hard-and-fast rules for joining a DAO, but being polite will probably go a long way.

An example of this evolution can be found in the experience of Alisha.ETH, who has emerged as one of the "personalities" in the Web3 space—and whose story will introduce us to the crucial aspect of entering the Web3 world. A New Zealander by birth, she went to law school and became an attorney after college, but the thought of being on the partner track for ten to fifteen years wasn't what she envisioned for herself. She felt it was more important to have a business where she could spend time with her husband, so she left to pursue a career in e-commerce. While she was running an online store, she was inadvertently introduced to the world of crypto when a customer asked to pay in Bitcoin. The woman was a regular customer to Alisha's Shopify store, so she just sent the woman her order and accepted Bitcoin without thinking. Two and a half years later, in 2017, the price of Bitcoin shot up, and the world had begun talking about crypto. By now, Alisha had what to her was a meaningful amount of crypto, and it piqued her interest. So she began to research it. She says she identified with the philosophy behind it, and from a practical perspective it made sense because she was using online payments for her business.

Alisha spent more time in the space, learning everything she could; she taught herself some front-end development so she could maintain her e-commerce store herself and save some money, and she started going to developer meetups. She began day-trading coins, and then, a year later, like a lot of people, she "got completely wiped out" when the price of cryptocurrencies tanked.

Alisha refocused her efforts on her e-commerce shop, but when COVID happened and New Zealand went into lockdown, she took time to pause, take stock, and decide what really excited her—what she wanted to spend her time doing. "And I kept coming back to crypto," she said. "I think that it's so much easier to do work when you believe at a fundamental level that it relates to the way that you should live your life." She wasn't a developer, nor did she have any aspirations to become one, so she tried to think of a way she could contribute to or participate in the space that made sense. In October 2020, Bitcoin experienced a bull run, with its price shooting up from around $10,000 to a high of almost $42,000 in January 2021. That's when she registered her ENS name: Alisha.ETH.

Alisha knew that ENS was an area she wanted to be involved in as soon as she learned that it was essentially the gateway protocol to Web3. ENS DAO's fund generates income from registration fees. When you register a dot ETH name, your $5 per year goes into the ENS DAO treasury. Alisha actually works for ENS Labs, a nonprofit incorporated in Singapore that launched at the end of 2021 in order to govern the protocol and to distribute and manage funds from the treasury. It's effectively the development team for the ENS protocol, funded by a grant from the DAO.

She thinks the idea that you should just drop into a DAO, work, and get paid for it misses the hugely important social aspect of these organizations—what she calls the human layer. "In my opinion," she says, "the human layer is like 80 percent of the DAO." When ENS DAO launched, there were only a handful of people on the team, including Alisha. "We launched what turned out to be a billion-dollar DAO in terms of the value of the community currency," she says. "There were two of us in the Discord overnight, and we watched it grow to three thousand members and then thirty thousand, and we were completely underwater." She said community members would drop into the Discord and begin offering support. "I felt like we were drowning, and they were throwing the buckets out, trying to get us back to being above water." That's the magic of DAOs, she says: community.

With that in mind, when you join a DAO for the first time, Alisha says you should treat onboarding like navigating a new country. Familiarize yourself with the terrain; understand the lay of the land—whether that's the technical aspect like the smart contracts or how the protocol works, or the social aspect. Are there working groups? Who are the people that hold the social capital in this environment? Where does the wealth in this country come from? What is the source of that wealth? Is it income from selling a product or service? Is it the value of the community currency when it's liquidated? And something that is vital after a period of time, after you've become familiar with the country, is to really ask yourself: Are you committed to being a citizen here, or are you just a tourist? People in the ENS community, she says, are definitely citizens. "ENS is the kind of place where people spend most of their time in crypto. Members are definitely not contributing across multiple DAOs."

Traditional companies are entering the Web3 space, and Alisha says ENS DAO has become an obvious jumping-off point. The fashion brand Puma, for example, has an ENS address. "They're really well placed to be early adopters of Web3 because it's in their culture and their blood that they are constantly innovating and pushing boundaries," Alisha said. "Their ENS name is a symbol of the fact that they understand what it means to be crypto native, to be part of the Ethereum ecosystem. And in doing so they can have a better relationship with their community. It's definitely a signal of their values." From a practical perspective, if they are doing any sort of drops—such as NFT drops related to limited-edition clothing capsules or event tickets— these can be highly effective for building community loyalty.

She explains that an ENS name is also an NFT, so it's possible for a fashion house to create a subdomain for event ticketing and drop NFTs to attendees. For example, Gucci might create a subdomain like paris2022.gucci.eth, and anyone who went to the Paris fashion show in 2022 would get distributed their own named subdomain, which is also an NFT that they can then hold in their wallet. It might have a customized avatar with their photo from the event. "There are all sorts of things you can do," Alisha says. "This crypto generation is really into experiences, and these kinds of things offer 'digital proof' they were there. If we go to the Eiffel Tower, it's not enough to take a picture and have it on your phone. You have to post it on Instagram or Twitter. So I think that same kind of logic applies—your wallet is so representative of your life experiences and who you are."

As Alisha's experience highlights, there really is no limit to what types of DAOs there can be and what they might enable—they are even changing how we have in-real-life (IRL) experiences. But this is only the tip of the iceberg: to really understand the true potential reach of DAOs, you need to know how they can impact the world.

CHAPTER SUMMARY:
How to Join a DAO

- The DAO environment is rapidly evolving. DAO involvement sometimes requires participants to hold community currencies for voting and necessitates doing your own up-to-date research before you get involved. Entry into these decentralized organizations varies, with different DAOs setting their own criteria ranging from open entry to formal interviews, and active social media presence can be beneficial.

- Joining a DAO, such as BanklessDAO or Gitcoin, entails specific processes, like entering a Discord server and contributing or submitting proposals and possibly going through interviews. It's crucial to research DAOs, understand their projects, and ensure alignment with your personal or career goals. Resources like job boards—such as the one on howtodao.xyz/jobs—can help you navigate opportunities.

- DAOs are inclusive, attracting diverse individuals from young developers to retirees, across various fields, all of whom are looking for a break from traditional ways of working. DAOs represent a world where organizations are about more than just turning a profit, instead embracing broader social, environmental, and cultural goals, and offering global participation regardless of geographical location, making them accessible for individuals who are dissatisfied with the limitations of the corporate world.

- ENS addresses, enabled by ENS DAO, are allowing brands and companies to create subdomains and NFT drops that coordinate with their physical experiences and products.

6

HOW TO USE DAOs
TO CREATE IMPACT

I f your goal is to change the world for the better, consider exploring impact DAOs. It may sound lofty to think that DAOs could revolutionize the worlds of science, medicine, environmental protection, humanitarian efforts, and more, but they are already showing potential in those spaces. Wherever extensive human coordination is required, DAOs have the ability to achieve great things.

VitaDAO

Take VitaDAO, which is focused on extending the human lifespan by funding and managing longevity research and therapies using blockchain technology. Members of VitaDAO contribute funds and, in return, receive the organization's native digital tokens. These tokens represent a form of governance share within the DAO, allowing holders to participate in decision-making processes, such as voting on which research proposals to fund and how to manage intellectual-property rights. The collaborative approach extends to the ownership and management of any resulting intellectual property, which remains within the VitaDAO ecosystem. This unique model is designed to ensure that discoveries and advancements are accessible and that therapies can be democratically distributed.

One lab that VitaDAO is supporting intends to use advanced machine learning to crunch the data from 1.04 billion medical prescriptions to understand the impact of drugs on the human lifespan. One of the core contributors to the DAO is Vincent Weisser. A product designer and software engineer, Vincent had followed the evolution of DAOs from the inception of The DAO through its failure and the resurrection of DAOs a couple of years later. He soon saw the opportunities for advancing scientific research and fixing what he calls "bigger problems." So Vincent started going to longevity conferences, teaching himself the basics of molecular biology.

Vincent and his cofounders knew that a conventional start-up wasn't the right structure for what they had in mind: start-ups usually have five or ten employees, and everyone needs to be paid. A nonprofit also felt limiting. Vincent said the team felt that the best structure was something that had an intimate community at its heart, one that encouraged people who wanted to participate. There was something very special about being part of a community that everyone was excited about—the Ethereum community, for example. The team realized that they could organize a DAO around raising money to fund important scientific research. VitaDAO met a need that Vincent said was apparent in medical science: later-stage clinical trials attract millions of dollars in funding, but there is less money available for earlier-stage trials. Vincent said one of the biggest funding bodies for US medical research is the National Institutes of Health (NIH), but it didn't fund much longevity research, and it had a much more bureaucratic process: a scientist might submit a sixty-page application, then wait half a year or a year to find out if it had been successful. By contrast, VitaDAO's process involved receiving a proposal (usually one or two pages) for a research project, discussing it on a call, and then making a decision on whether to fund it or not.

The community has around ten thousand members in the forum and two thousand token holders. Some members who do not own tokens still participate by giving comments. Scientists share interesting research, but there are people in the DAO who contribute a lot of time to make research happen even if they're not researchers themselves. Some of the members have an MD or a PhD, or they want to be involved simply because they understand the importance of the work being done. Some may contribute to the fund; others contribute time and expertise. The power, Vincent said, is this combination of both capital and expertise coming together and informing what particular research to fund. The core idea behind VitaDAO is to help reduce the burden of health care and age-related diseases, which are the biggest health and financial burdens on society. Vincent says the ambition of longevity research is to solve diseases like cancer and dementia more efficiently by identifying their root causes. And longevity research aims to address these common factors in order to find solutions for multiple diseases simultaneously. As a result, if we lived to the age of ninety but remained as healthy as a fifty-year-old, it would have significant benefits for society.

The research-review process essentially involves a researcher sending in a proposal, after which experienced researchers from different backgrounds evaluate this research. Those evaluations are visible to the members of the community, who can then vote based on the pros and cons of that research, the market, and its potential. The community can also delegate their votes to trusted scientists or enthusiasts. The trick is to break down the reviews into easy-to-understand language so that everyone can learn from them. Vincent says Pfizer is also on board and makes comments in the governance room. He says watching the communication and discussion happening in the open is captivating: "Scientists are not all-knowing, so the fascinating thing is following the discussions because you see people who have been in the field for twenty years talking to people who have been in the field for forty years talking to a fresh researcher. Have you tried out this? Oh, this looks inconclusive. You should try that. Should we scrap the research because this looks really promising instead? And sometimes even the researchers who are some of the most reputable in the field don't have these ideas that some of the community members might have. I think that's really the power."

VitaDAO's approach addresses several challenges in traditional biomedical research and development, including funding limitations, bureaucratic inefficiencies, and the often prohibitive cost of accessing cutting-edge treatments. Big Pharma is motivated by turning a profit for investors. It has a fiduciary duty to do what's best for those investors to maximize their return, even if that means a cost to the public. Pharmaceutical companies rely on the bureaucratic funding infrastructure to stamp out competition, it takes a lot of administrative overheads to manage all of this bureaucracy, and that keeps innovators from challenging their market positions. Depending on where in the world you live, you might see medicine prices skyrocket, or you might see the sale of drugs that pharmaceutical companies know aren't effective—or that may even be dangerous—but the profits are higher than the fines the companies would have to pay if they were found out (if they're in a regulated market at all).

The World-Changing Potential of DAOs

But this is just the tip of the iceberg. Currently, DAOs are being used to fund disaster-relief efforts. They can be used to manage the distribution of humanitarian aid and to provide microfinance loans to people in developing countries. DAOs can fund environmental and climate initiatives that have been selected through a community-driven voting process, meaning that only the most promising and impactful projects receive funding. DAOs can use blockchain technology to track carbon-offset credits, support sustainable agriculture practices, and fund organizations that work to protect endangered species. Through these and other possible efforts, DAOs have the potential to effect change on a global scale.

Part of why this can be so effective—even more effective than traditional ways of doing this kind of work—is the collective, collaborative nature of how DAOs operate. If a lot of people want to contribute in order to change something for the better, that motivates others to do the same, creating a positive loop that DAOs are perfectly suited to capitalize on. For proof, just look at the incredibly large treasuries of some DAOs. As of early 2024, Optimism DAO's treasury is comparable to the GDP of a small country such as Andorra or Sierra Leone.

In fact, we believe there is a strong chance that DAOs will become the largest funding mechanisms for public goods that the planet has ever seen. Public goods are goods or services that are provided to all people for their benefit, like the roads we ride on or the open-source software that developers use free of charge for their applications. DAOs are an ideal place to evolve public goods because they often have treasuries and public goods to fund (software development, community education, or other things that are available to all participants in the ecosystem). A public-goods funding mechanism is a set of rules or a process encoded into a smart contract that determines which public goods to fund and how much. The transparency and efficiency inherent to smart contracts built on crypto ensure that those who give will know, and influence, how their money is spent—unlike in most traditional philanthropic efforts and organizations—not to mention what happens to your taxes. Crypto offers the ability to do more scalable, precise, democratic capital allocation in a way that was not possible before we had programmable smart contracts.

One example of how this might work is Molecule, a Berlin-based company that has created an NFT wrapper for intellectual property, allowing for more transparent and liquid markets in what is traditionally a very opaque and difficult area for nonaccredited investors to buy and sell. Researchers can now sell off a portion of their intellectual property in the form of "fractionalized NFTs" and use the funds for further research. The value of the intellectual property represented by the NFT increases as more research is conducted, making it even more valuable. The use of smart contracts allows for permissionless management and distribution of the intellectual property to NFT owners. This eliminates the need for traditional biotech VCs and institutional investors, making it easier to sell the intellectual property to pharma companies and distribute profits proportionately to NFT owners.

We already see DAOs accomplishing multiple things: fundraising for existing projects, designing projects from scratch, and funding them all within the DAO. However, a DAO might not be the best way to execute some of the work itself, so it can also be used to fundraise and then outsource projects to local companies. For example, Big Green DAO—founded by Kimbal Musk, Elon's brother—is working on problems of food scarcity by making grants to nonprofits that specialize in those problems. In each case the DAO might identify where the biggest problems are that need tackling and find local resources to tackle those issues on the ground while the DAO focuses on fundraising and prioritizing projects.

But DAOs won't just impact how we implement projects in the world: they could also revolutionize the way that we research and develop life-changing discoveries. Sharing information is a hallmark of DAOs, but in the old-fashioned centralized model of doing science, proprietary research is secret. Information is to be protected, not shared. Protecting your IP, though, is something the blockchain can solve technically. If you have some valuable IP data, you can store a record of your ownership onchain, and nobody can see the actual data that record contains unless you give them permission. And if they want it, and you want them to have it, either they need to pay for it or you can give it away—but the point is it's your choice, and the identity of the person (you) who came up with the idea is set in stone because the ownership structure is transparent.

It's perhaps easier to imagine this concept by using a piece of art. Let's say I create a picture and put it on the blockchain and sell it. I'll make the initial money from that sale, but because there's an immutable record of me having created it, I'll also get royalties when it's resold. My relationship to that piece of art is encoded so that whenever a resale happens, I'll still get those royalties. And because of the code, I'll know whenever someone resells my piece or art or reuses my invention. Because of this, scientists will be more willing not just to share their knowledge but also to contribute to solutions. Boris Dyakov, a PhD candidate in molecular genetics who is also involved in the "decentralized science" space, explains it like this: intellectual property in biotech and biopharma is usually protected by trade secrets and patents, but in the United States, at least, enforcement of these patents is possible only through legal means and sanctions imposed by the government.

In impact DAOs specifically, the concept of governance tokens can often be better understood as a donation, or a "ticket to the movement," since these tokens have no monetary value and are essentially worthless from a fiduciary perspective. Therefore, many impact DAOs,

DAOs that focus on positive change in the world, are more of a charity or foundation than a typical investment organization.

The plan with VitaDAO is, of course, to grow the treasury—for example, it might sell its research to other biotech companies—but if it does, that money will always be reinvested into funding more research. Vincent puts it like this: "If you put $1 million into curing cancer and it turns into $10m because some of your cancer research was successful, of course you want to fund more cancer research. Ultimately that's the goal of the majority of the community."

This doesn't have to stop at merely raising and channeling capital, though. For those parts of the world where you can't even open a bank account or get a loan greater than a few hundred dollars, DAOs offer the opportunity to change the very nature of entrepreneurship.

One of the most exciting examples of this kind of forward-thinking change is Pando DAO. Pando DAO could also be considered an investment DAO, which we'll cover in more detail later, but its mission makes it feel very relevant to illustrating the breadth and variety of what impact DAOs can be. It's named after the Pando aspen grove in Utah, a forest connected by a single root system, and it aims to build a more connected tech community on the African continent and help its members through investment and collaboration. It's the brainchild of Yacob Berhane, an American of Eritrean descent who decided to move to Africa a decade ago. His grandfather had graduated from Harvard, but Berhane felt duty bound to return to Eritrea to help build his country following the first war for independence from Ethiopia. Berhane's grandfather became a judge but was assassinated for trying to instill democracy. After he graduated from Howard, the younger Berhane worked as a debt originator; he lived in America and could see the path to creating a pretty comfortable life for himself. But he thought about his grandfather and the sacrifices he had made.

Berhane started working to help African tech entrepreneurs and start-ups grow. Before long, his name got out as someone who could help founders raise funds. The problem wasn't that African entrepreneurs weren't smart or gritty; it was just that they didn't speak the same capitalistic language as the Western world does. Berhane thought, "I know that language. So let me transfer that language over to them so that way they're able to receive the resources they need."

Berhane created Pariti, which helped early-stage African start-ups raise capital. But Pariti was a for-profit start-up—an African parallel to, say, AngelList. What Berhane began to realize was that he had access to an immense amount of information and resources. He recognized there was a significant knowledge gap between himself and others that could lead to unnecessary mistakes and setbacks for those without the same level of access. And he began to understand that this ecosystem of founders understood that it was much greater than any one of them, that they were all codependent. Even if someone was competing with you, you needed them to be successful. So he decided to create a community for founders to connect and share information with one another. He brought all the founders he knew together into a single group chat, allowing for more collaborative and efficient communication. This was the beginning of Pando DAO—an evolution, of sorts, of Pariti. Some DAOs use Discord; Berhane chose to use WhatsApp. Berhane soon discovered that in his group chat he had eighty-eight founders who together represented over $5 billion in start-up valuation, a quarter billion in direct foreign capital investment into their start-ups, and more than seventeen thousand employees across sixteen countries.

So what distinguishes Pando DAO from just a WhatsApp group of like-minded people? They had a shared bank account, for one. And each person's vote—whether on DAO governance issues or which project to fund—would be represented by tokens. Like most DAOs, Pando DAO rewards its members for their contributions. If you're too busy to contribute, you'll have fewer tokens. Berhane, who inevitably contributes most to the DAO, has his power "neutralized" through quadratic voting, in order to maintain equality and fairness. "It's destructive for a DAO if one person has too much power," he says. "And I can't pass anything alone because I have three other members with me on the treasury committee and I need their votes too."

Pando DAO's first task, though, was to raise a $20m fund: a venture-capital (VC) fund within the DAO. They would then be able to invest in African founders, and all the other founders in Pando DAO would have a duty and responsibility to help those founders. It would go from being a space where founders could run their ideas by innovators and builders in the community, receiving feedback and guidance from experienced individuals who understand the challenges of being an entrepreneur, to one that would also fund these start-ups, giving Pando's members a vested interest in the success of the start-ups it supports. "The reason why it works better in a DAO?" Berhane says. "If I just said, 'Hey man, you should help the next generation of founders,' you might not take action because you have no skin in the game. But if I said, 'Hey, you should help them because your token is tied to the returns of the fund—so these founders in the DAO can actually make money,' it'd be a different story."

Berhane said he and the other founders in Pando DAO knew these people seeking help from the DAO were about to go through. They had the knowledge to tell them: don't incorporate there; don't design that tax policy; don't hire through that contract because that's going to be a mistake that really messed things up for us. This was about founders transferring their knowledge to the next founders. It was about reciprocity and paying it forward.

Berhane acknowledges that many people are skeptical of crypto, but he believes that the potential rewards outweigh the risks, especially in certain African countries where economic activity needs to increase. Crypto, he believes, offers an efficient infrastructure with low fees and protection against inflation, making it a valuable tool for promoting economic growth. Berhane says accessing credit across the African continent for small and medium-sized enterprises and businesses is tough.

Once Pando raises a fund, the DAO can invest in the next generation of African start-ups. To qualify for membership in Pando, a founder must be working on an African start-up and have raised at least $2 million. Berhane believes that founders who have raised this amount have a common set of experiences and problems, such as finding product-market fit and figuring out taxes and contracts for hiring. Once a fund is established, entrepreneurs pitch the fund. Founders in the DAO with relevant experience will screen the pitch—the founder of an established health-care start-up would screen a pitch for a new health-care start-up, for example—after which Pando DAO members will vote on whether to invest. They'll use a "20 percent rule"—meaning that 20 percent of members need to vote. These are founders, Berhane says, and they have companies to run, so they're incredibly busy. Based on the outcome of that vote, the fund would then allocate capital to the project. That start-up might raise a million dollars. But if it raises $2 million, its founder is immediately eligible to join the DAO as a member—not just a beneficiary of its investment. They will then pay it forward.

"Ultimately," Berhane says, "I think the best thing we can do at Pando is to show economic returns on this activity. Because the altruistic stuff is great, but people need to eat food, people need to have jobs, insurance, access to bank accounts and financial services. It's hard to tell someone a lofty idea who is starving. No one cares about your wallet if you're not able to show that you can create jobs; no one cares if you're not able to show that you can bring down the cost of maize. If you're not able to show that you can increase access to drugs and health care, no one cares."

QUEST 5: Fund projects through a DAO.

If you're excited about the prospect of making an impact with DAOs, then you can get started immediately: find a DAO that's engaged with a cause that you believe is meaningful and get involved!

One easy way to do this is through Gitcoin Grants. Check out grants.gitcoin.co and fund what matters to you. Or just browse around and see just how many causes DAOs are taking on.

As always, you can find detailed instructions at howtodao.xyz/quest.

CHAPTER SUMMARY:
How to Use DAOs to Create Impact

- Impact DAOs are emerging as a transformative force in sectors like health care, environmental protection, and humanitarian aid, decentralizing funding and decision-making processes to address global issues more efficiently and transparently.

- Projects like VitaDAO demonstrate the practical applications of DAOs, from funding longevity research and collaboratively managing intellectual property to ensuring drug authenticity and supply-chain integrity through blockchain technology.

- DAOs facilitate global coordination on pressing issues such as climate change and disaster relief, enabling community-driven funding, problem-solving, and efficient resource allocation, potentially becoming one of the largest funding mechanisms for public goods.

- Impact DAOs are among our favorite types of DAOs because they are genuinely changing the world we live in. They are driven not by profit but by the impact they aim to create for all of us. Even if this is not something you want to personally pursue, you should consider supporting impact DAOs in other ways, such as through donations on Gitcoin Grants. Remember, every contribution, even as little as one dollar, counts, thanks to the quadratic funding mechanism.

7

HOW TO USE DAOs
TO GET PAID

reating impact is far from the only way to participate in DAOs. If your reason for getting involved with a DAO is to advance your career, participate in the growing Web3/crypto ecosystem, or just to make some money, then there are plenty of DAOs for that as well.

In this chapter we will lift the veil around financial remuneration, explaining these decentralized entities, drawing parallels and contrasts with more traditional organizations. Just like in those conventional organizations, where payment structures might range from work for hire to stable employment, or even entrepreneurial revenue sharing, DAOs adopt these diverse models.

Some DAOs pay in ETH or USD-equivalent tokens. Others pay in their native-community currency. Governance tokens within a DAO grant decision-making power, rewarding active contributors by amplifying their voice in those decisions. These tokens can act as community currencies. Although contributors may sell their tokens, they also have the option to retain them, even leveraging them for borrowing if they really believe in a project, thereby covering their expenses without selling their stake.

Many DAOs pay in their community currencies, and there is an economy around that. Central banks can print money, which will devalue your currency; if you join a DAO that has its own currency, however, you'll be part of a community that is essentially controlling its own currency on a micro level. This presents both opportunity and risk.

Before we dive into the DAO economy, let's take a look at how the traditional economy works. Most economies are controlled by two key powers: monetary policy and fiscal policy. Fiscal policy is determined by the government, often focusing on taxation and fund redistribution. Monetary policy is directed by central banks, such as the US Federal Reserve, and it influences interest rates and controls how much money is in circulation. While most countries maintain control over fiscal policy, a few opt to outsource monetary policy to establish a more robust economic framework—such as the European Union, where most of the countries use the euro instead of their national currency; the euro is controlled by the European Central Bank. There are several reasons to use this approach: a common currency streamlines international business by eliminating exchange-rate risks, and a larger (and stronger) economic body is generally more stable.

Despite the prevailing trend among nation-states to outsource monetary policy and adopt shared currencies like the euro or dollar, DAOs have taken the opposite route. Nearly every DAO has control over its own monetary policy. It can issue a token that can be used to vote on the DAO's governance and sometimes can be traded for goods and services outside of its ecosystem (a token is said to have "liquidity" if you can trade it for other assets). During the bull run, this capability was particularly beneficial, as token prices experienced notable surges. Although the bear market presented challenges, resulting in a significant decline in the value of many DAOs, it was a crucial learning experience. It underscored how dynamic DAO monetary strategies can be in the face of market volatility, especially for smaller entities with lower liquidity.

The stability of a community's currency can be established by a high income; a DAO that doesn't receive any monetary inflows but has many community currencies may not hold any significant value, whereas a DAO that has millions of dollars of inflows and a fixed supply of currency may see its community currency be very valuable and appreciate over time. But one of the strengths of Web3 is that this isn't the only way to create a business model. Every DAO can create its own economic system and unique business model, providing different paths to stability and growth.

Envisaging the future, we anticipate that DAOs will adopt a diverse array of monetary models to navigate effectively through varied market scenarios. Some DAOs might share currencies, emulating the European Union's model, while others may leverage stable nation-state currencies, like the dollar, to circumvent market fluctuations. In the spirit of innovation, it is expected that DAOs will also devise entirely new financial approaches, continuing to explore and define the financial landscape of decentralized autonomous organizations.

If you are going to accept payment in the currency of a DAO you work for, be sure to do extensive research on the viability of the project. You may be paid in a volatile cryptocurrency—which can be a lot of fun on the upside but not a lot of fun on the downside.

Because of these factors, the DAO ecosystem may present fewer administrative hurdles and offer swifter transactions with less paperwork. Many DAOs aspire to the tenet that every contributor is compensated according to their input and the prevailing financial health of the organization. Overall, there are four main types of payment:

1. **BOUNTY SYSTEM**—finish the task, and you'll get paid for it.
2. **EARN PROTOCOL-BASED REWARDS**—many DAOs revolve around a protocol. Learn how the protocol works and then earn from it.

3. **FIXED PAYMENT OR SALARY**—you're hired for this number of hours, and this is how much you'll get paid.

4. **COMMUNITY DISTRIBUTION**—members of the DAO decide together who should get paid based on how much they contributed.

Let's get into each of these in more detail.

BOUNTY SYSTEM

A "bounty board" is typically a system or platform where various tasks, projects, or objectives are posted, usually by the organization's members or governance mechanisms, each associated with a specific reward or "bounty." These bounties are incentivized, often in the form of cryptocurrencies, provided in exchange for the completion of the task or project listed on the board.

Here's how this generally works in a DAO context:

- **TASK LISTING:** Tasks are defined by members of the DAO or through collective agreement (often reached through proposals and voting mechanisms inherent to the DAO). These tasks can range widely, from development work to marketing, community management, content creation, and more.

- **BOUNTY ALLOCATION:** Each task on the bounty board will have a bounty associated with it, set aside as an incentive for completion. The bounty's size can depend on the task's perceived difficulty, the task's importance, or the level of skill required to complete it.

- **OPEN PARTICIPATION AND COMPLETION:** Depending on the DAO's rules, either members of the DAO or anyone can select a task and work on it. This process embodies the principle of decentralized collaboration, which is fundamental to many DAOs.

- **REVIEW AND REWARD DISBURSEMENT:** Once a task is completed, there's usually a review process, conducted by designated members of the community, to ensure that the task meets the required standards or objectives. If the output is accepted, the bounty is released to the individual or team that completed the work.

- **TRANSPARENCY AND TRACEABILITY:** All these interactions (task postings, acceptances, completion verifications, and transactions) are typically conducted on the blockchain that hosts the DAO, ensuring that they are transparent, traceable, and immutable. This openness is vital to building trust among participants and is integral to the functioning of DAOs.

The DAO's bounty board represents a microcosm of the broader gig economy, driven by decentralized decision-making, and it often attracts a global pool of talent. It's a flexible way for DAOs to achieve goals and milestones without the need to hire employees in a traditional sense, adhering instead to their decentralized, often libertarian principles of operation. Bounties are a great way to get your foot in the door at a DAO.

EARN PROTOCOL-BASED REWARDS

Many DAOs are centered around a particular protocol, the foundational rules or code that governs the activity on a blockchain. For instance, the Uniswap DAO is built around the Uniswap protocol, while the Gitcoin DAO revolves around Gitcoin Grants and the Optimism DAO is based on the Optimism chain.

By familiarizing yourself with each protocol in the space, you can identify opportunities to generate income by leveraging the unique strengths of each protocol.

For example, the Gitcoin protocol enables you to secure funding for your next idea through grants. On the other hand, Uniswap has a stronger focus on trading, allowing you to provide liquidity to the protocol and receive trading fees. Furthermore, Optimism regularly conducts airdrops and retroactive public goods funding rounds, providing rewards for active participation in the ecosystem and for building on top of the protocol.

FIXED PAYMENT OR SALARY

In traditional organizations, salaried payments are straightforward: employees receive a fixed payment from the employer. However, DAO structures are nontraditional because of the decentralized and often global nature of participants, and the mechanisms for regular "salaried" payments, if they exist, can be quite different.

First, for someone to receive a salary or any type of payment, the DAO's members must typically agree to the terms. This agreement is often reached through a proposal process where the prospective salaried individual or team submits a detailed plan for their role, responsibilities, and requested compensation. The DAO members vote on this proposal, and if it gains enough support, it is approved.

DAOs can then execute these agreements in two different ways. Salaries in DAOs can be managed through programmable smart contracts on the blockchain. Once the terms are agreed upon, a smart contract can be set to automatically execute these payments at regular intervals (e.g., monthly) in the agreed-upon cryptocurrency. The conditions of employment and payment are thus both transparent and immutable, encoded in the blockchain.

Or you can use contribution-based models. Some DAOs adopt a more flexible, contribution-based model for compensation, which can resemble a regular salary but is based on ongoing contributions. For instance, a core contributor to a DAO might receive regular compensation, adjusted based on their input and the evolving needs and resources of the DAO. In some cases, especially if the salaries require flexibility based on changing conditions, funds for salaries might be held in a multisignature wallet, a kind of cryptocurrency wallet designed to add an extra layer of protection for assets that could be stolen using only one password or wallet key. Disbursement of these funds requires the approval of several designated DAO members, providing a form of checks and balances.

All DAOs are subject to laws, so the next step is to make sure you comply with local regulations. Because DAOs operate globally and most countries have regulations regarding employment, taxes, and more, individuals receiving regular compensation through a DAO must typically manage their compliance and tax obligations. But since transactions on the blockchain are transparent, payments are visible, ensuring accountability. This setup can help prevent fraud or unfair payment practices because all members can see and, if necessary, contest transactions.

Last, it's important to remember that a "salary" in a DAO does not come with traditional employment benefits (such as health insurance and retirement) unless specifically outlined in the proposal and agreement. For tax and legal purposes, DAO participants are usually considered independent contractors or freelancers. Also, because DAOs are a relatively new and rapidly evolving concept, best practices and standard procedures are still in development within the crypto and legal communities.

COMMUNITY DISTRIBUTION

Distributing rewards via community distribution can get complicated quickly. Rewarding each member or establishing distribution criteria can morph into a complex endeavor; maintaining a record of all member activities, understanding how each contribution impacts overarching goals, and monitoring individual contributors become increasingly difficult, particularly as the DAO expands. Distributing rewards necessitates a substantial management effort and presents scaling challenges—but fortunately there are tools to make it easier.

Coordinape is a software platform designed to address that problem by quickly and fairly distributing those resources to contributors. It's a way of having the whole community of working contributors decide compensation in an open and transparent way. Let's use BanklessDAO as an example. Each month, every single member of Bankless gets tokens to vote on who contributed the most to the DAO and what payment they should receive. Essentially, there's a pile of money each month to be distributed to DAO contributors. And each month, members of that DAO will vote on who gets what, depending on their contributions. Each contributor is given a number of "gift tokens" based on their level or rank within the DAO. Let's say you get a hundred tokens—

you then use these to reward people who you know to have contributed substantially to the DAO. Each token represents a portion of the total compensation budget that is going to be distributed, and once everyone has distributed their votes, contributors are paid in proportion to the votes each has received. So instead of your boss determining your compensation, it's your peers. And vice versa: you determine your boss's compensation!

So how does this actually work? Let's explore by looking at Coordinape. Tracheopteryx (his Web3 name) launched Coordinape, which thousands of people in DAOs are now using in order to solve workers' compensation. *Tracheopteryx*—Trach for short—is an artistic pastiche: a portmanteau of *trachea*, the organ of human song and speech, and *Archaeopteryx*, the first feathered dinosaur. It's fitting. Trach says we're in a period of phase change in human coordination where our collective structures are no longer serving us. Trach was on the cusp of that phase change with Yearn, a decentralized finance protocol he worked for, and now Coordinape. Trach had been tracking crypto since 2010, but he never really got deep into it until the DeFi Summer, a period of explosive growth for decentralized finance in the summer of 2020 that attracted mainstream attention and was characterized by surging token prices and massive trading.

"What really pulled me in was the emergence of DAOs," Trach says. "There were large volumes of financial movement happening with groups of strangers around the world, using arcane voting techniques to come to consensus, and I was like, wow, I gotta get me some of this."

Trach had run several different businesses before and had hired staff and run large teams, but he was always unhappy with how that process worked: "You can't get away from the fact that all decisions flow up to you and then you have to tell people what to do, and so I tried to do it differently; I tried to give ownership of one of my companies to other people in the company, but that didn't go super well, so I was drawn to this notion that maybe there was a better way."

The better way was DAOs. At the core was supposed to be "decentralized coordination," but what Trach initially saw was disorganization. "It was like the most chaotic thing ever," he says. "The analogy that comes to mind is of a primordial soup; it was all these people—all these molecules and ions—bumping into one another in some kind of superheated gas. There have been a lot of cases like this throughout history where there were worker collectives, but they didn't have the same foundation of value capture. In DAOs there was all this money flowing in, which allows for a totally different level of activity and energy. So I saw that, and I was captivated, and I knew I just had to be part of it."

Trach was a key early contributor to Yearn, which was a pioneer of decentralized finance. Built on top of the Ethereum blockchain, Yearn has been described as "an Amazon marketplace for interest-bearing crypto products," allowing investors to lend, borrow, and earn on their assets. Then he helped develop Coordinape, a tool that would help DAO members decide who was contributing and who wasn't, and that would then enable token drops to pay them.

Coordinape quickly became one of the most effective and successful coordination tools in the DAO ecosystem. Trach says he always aimed to be somebody who put principles before money, and once he'd discovered DAOs and their enormous potential, he wanted to figure out a way to enable members of those DAOs to get paid more easily.

"It was like we had this persistent problem whereby we had all these people trying to do something well—and also money coming in—but as soon as there was money coming in, then people fought about it. There were rivalries; there were coalitions," Trach says. "And so you had real, tangible governance to solve there. So it's been tension-driven. There were practical operational needs from the beginning, and that is what you want in order to design the system. So we designed a whole new system of architecture and of governance we called 'constrained delegation.' It's a kind of delegated governance where instead of delegating your voting power, you vote to delegate decision-making power to autonomous teams that can act on behalf of the DAO."

Trach says one of the really persistent challenges in decentralized work is how compensation is handled: "Most of the time you've got grant mechanisms—old ideas like salary, stock vesting, equity, but we needed something new. We needed something that was DAO native. We wanted to create fair, asymmetric value allocation between groups of decentralized workers without a top-down process." Trach also knew it had to be competitive with other systems, particularly if another system of compensation was going to attract more people. "And if that's a top-down, rigid, hierarchical system, but it rewards people better, that's going to win in the near term," he says, "and so we had to compete with that for talent."

How does Coordinape work, and how did it solve the sort of problems that Trach had identified? In the early days at Yearn, in terms of "staff" they had a few people who were pretty much working full-time—their compensation streams were settled—but then there were a lot of other people who were contributing a good deal but in a part-time context. So Trach and his colleagues established a small group of recurring grants that began as gifts: "We just thought: we've got money, we had the operational proposal to give away some money, and so every month we'd say, hey, who's been doing cool stuff? She has; he has; they have. And so we'd award $3,000 here, $2,000 there. We'd just give money away as a gift. It was not a quid pro quo agreement. And it was great; it was really powerful. But what we found pretty quickly after a few months was that it took a lot of work and we didn't feel like we were particularly good at it.

"If you look at the theories of work," Trach says, "the wisdom is at the edges of these types of networks. It's a lot harder to create a fair allocation from the center or the top or the bottom, but it's better to do it from the edges. In other words, the actual people doing the work often know best the value of that work. And so that was the inspiration for Coordinape."

He says that although Coordinape has evolved over time, it was initially inspired by the idea of gift economies, an anthropological concept defined by Merriam-Webster as "a system in which goods and services are given freely between people rather than sold or bartered"—what he calls "pay-it-forward" ideas. "While Coordinape is a compensation system," Trach says, "I think people get a little confused thinking that the money is the gift. It's not. The money is essentially the symbolic bracelet. The 'gift' is the work itself, the work that people give to the community."

The great thing about the "gift circle" is, Trach says, that it can be totally decentralized. "With a circle of people, every month you can go through this gift ceremony in which every member of the circle receives, say, a hundred tokens. And the token is a kind of database artifact, like a poker chip. You're not allowed to keep them. You have to give them away, and they only have value if you give them away. This also references back to gift economies, where the notion of wealth was reversed; the people that gave the most were considered the most wealthy. So you give away your hundred poker chips, or gift tokens, and the idea—the 'ask'—is this: who have you directly seen create value in this community? And when you've identified them, you give them a symbol of your appreciation through these tokens."

Trach believes we don't have to have golden handcuffs to keep us interested in something; we don't need to be peer-pressured into working in the ways we once did, with a carrot-and-stick approach. Instead, we should be able to sense what our calling is in the world or what our gifts are, and we should be able to offer those to our communities and then get rewarded for that work by our peers. If you want to take a month off and travel around Patagonia, you should simply be able to talk to the people you're working with and go.

"I can imagine this kind of nomad worker who doesn't have to have any contracts with anybody," Trach says. "She can work as much or as little as she wants. And when she puts work out into this system, she can get rewarded through overlapping gift circles from different communities, by her peers and admirers and colleagues. And she can work for five DAOs at once if she wants to. Or one DAO."

QUEST 6: Earn some tokens.

As you dive deeper into DAOs, you should start to see ways of earning tokens within individual communities, whether it's through job boards or any of the other methods listed above. Earning tokens is a way of being rewarded for your time and really becoming a part of a DAO's ecosystem, and it will help you take the next step in your DAO journey.

Not sure where to start? Check out our curated job board at howtodao.xyz/jobs.

As always, you can find detailed instructions at howtodao.xyz/quest.

Even with fixed salaries, DAO environments often dissolve the conventional 9-to-5 structure, endorsing flexible hours to accommodate the global nature of their operations. Your association is not driven purely by the paycheck. Instead, it revolves around a genuine desire to collaborate, contribute to the mission, and innovate alongside like-minded individuals. Despite potential variations in earnings, the collective progress of the team could lead to an appreciation of your tokens, potentially boosting your salary. The bounty system provides freelancers or individuals transitioning into Web3 with an excellent avenue to gain experience and earn, and it enables DAOs' flexibility. And the community distribution enables DAOs with any budget to coordinate with a large number of contributors and ensure that everyone is fairly compensated for their involvement.

Initially, DAOs were able to attract new recruits by simply being the in-vogue thing: the hot new arrival on the tech scene. Established "old world" companies and organizations were busy offering benefits to lure good candidates: more vacation time, amazing health insurance, stock options. But as DAOs matured, they realized that they, too, needed to offer additional incentives in order to remain competitive. Today, most pay at least 15 percent above market rate, and more and more are offering benefits like health insurance and paid leave and converting your crypto earnings to cash.

Inevitably, with anything new in the digital space, there will be kinks that need working out. The space is still evolving. Sustainability is a concern. Job security is a concern. Volatility is a concern. With the speed at which the DAO ecosystem is moving, it's easy to forget stuff like this. In traditional companies it takes time to get hired, and it can take even more time to fire someone because of safeguards that are in place. DAOs are not like that: you can get hired on the spot, but you can also lose your role overnight. These transitions can be stressful if you're not used to them, but the upside is that you don't need to go through a three-month-long interview process to get back on your feet again. You can simply join another DAO—instantly. There are many people who work for several DAOs at a time, a plural approach that is anti-fragile, symbiotic to changes in roles. Working for a DAO—possibly as a digital nomad—can be an isolating experience for some. But projects are popping up everywhere to address this and to support the ecosystem. The environment's still evolving, but the good thing is the community can see what's needed to ensure that it succeeds and there are people working to address those issues. Decentralization doesn't mean we should only take care of ourselves; it means we should take care of each other.

How to Get Benefits While Working at a DAO: Opolis

Perhaps understandably, some people working full-time for DAOs found it hard to go to their bank and borrow money: try telling a teller at your local credit union that you'd like a mortgage and that you work for a decentralized autonomous organization that exists on the blockchain. Luckily, there are now services that can help. Opolis is one of them. It was set up to allow independent workers such as freelancers, gig workers, and DAO contributors to access benefits like medical insurance and retirement plans that are typically reserved for employees of traditional corporations. Some services will help you create an LLC so that the DAO you're working for will appear as part of a corporate entity, and you can then access a W2 showing your annual income, confirmation of employment, benefits, and insurance.

Joshua Lapidus, a founding steward of Opolis, likes to joke about the awkward transaction that inevitably happens when someone working in crypto, for DAOs, or really anywhere in that space needs to go to the bank. "You walk in and say 'I make magic internet money from a magic internet community,' and the banker says, 'Jog on.'"

That's where Opolis comes in. The vision was to provide a service broader than just for DAOs. Joshua says the American Dream is a concept of rugged individualism and breaking down societal barriers so that there's social mobility, but that every single incentive, every piece of messaging from the government, is that you need to subjugate yourself to the man in order to have the best life possible. Joshua thinks these are competing narratives: you can get the best rates on health care, retirement benefits, and incentives, but only if you work for a Fortune 500 company. So the best possible way to succeed in life is to subjugate yourself to somebody else and be the workhorse for them. He says the core premise of Opolis is that every single person should be a sovereign individual who wraps themself in a company that Opolis calls "an employment vehicle" and then is able to lease their time and attention to whichever organization they want.

"So instead of working from nine to five, sitting working in a chair for forty hours a week for the man, we look at it like this: a lot of companies don't need you for forty hours. Maybe they only need you for thirty, and so they should be paying you for that time so that you can go and spend that other ten or twenty working on other things." Opolis takes all the individuals who've applied to be members of its employment DAO and groups them into its cooperative. Opolis is essentially the service provider for that DAO. And when people join, they borrow the strength of the DAO: strength in numbers. Opolis then negotiates with a broker to get better rates for health insurance—Joshua says in 90 percent of states it's a pretty significant discount—and dental and vision coverage, both of which are significantly better than what you can get on the exchange. "And that's because we negotiate five hundred to one, whereas on the exchange you're negotiating one to one. So it's this group-buying power."

Joshua says the organization is able to scale this infinitely, and much faster than a company could because neither Opolis nor the employment DAO is paying the salaries. Each individual pays her own salary through the DAO. Here's how it works: if you're a freelancer wanting to join the employment DAO, you'll contribute 1 percent of your earnings. But Joshua points out that the 1 percent is not a fee that's going to shareholders or some executive board. You're becoming a member—an owner—of the cooperative. And once there are more people paying that 1 percent, there will eventually be profits to distribute. The goal is to maximize benefits to the DAO members and minimize costs to the DAO members.

Opolis is able to take your 1099 freelance income and convert it into W2 income with pay stubs. So instead of telling the tax man, "Taxes have not been withheld yet, so charge me self-employment taxes," the W2 is telling him that your employer withheld a portion of federal, state, and local withholding taxes, even Social Security and Medicare. And you can take that W2 to any lender, and they'll view you as a less risky borrower—because it looks like you're working for a company rather than for yourself. Opolis also pays into workers' compensation and unemployment insurance, so Joshua says if you lose your job at the DAO and you don't have any income coming in before you find your next role, you're actually able to draw from unemployment insurance. Or if you have an accident, you can get workers' comp.

DAOs may only be a handful of years old, but already organizations like Opolis are springing up to meet the inevitable challenges and hurdles along the way.

CHAPTER SUMMARY:
How to Use DAOs to Get Paid

- **ENCOURAGING ENTREPRENEURSHIP:** DAOs emphasize a peer-to-peer compensation model, fostering an entrepreneurial spirit and ensuring equitable value distribution.

- **MONETARY POLICY IN DAOs:** DAOs intertwine governance with monetary policy through tokens representing power and potential transactional value.

- **SHARED SUCCESS IN DAOs:** DAO structures harmonize individual and group achievements, aligning motivations with the organization's goals.

- **BENEFITS IN DAOs:** Services like Opolis are enabling workers at DAOs to now receive benefits as well by using "employment vehicles" to unite independent contractors.

8

HOW TO USE DECENTRALIZED FINANCE

Before you engage with the multiplayer world of investing with DAOs, it can be helpful to do some single-player exploration. Anyone who has played video games probably knows the meanings of *single player* and *multiplayer*—*single player* means you're playing alone, whereas *multiplayer* means you're playing with other people. Once you understand that, you can see how DAOs are basically crypto in multiplayer mode.

The potential of community currencies extends beyond mere access and governance. Some have financial value, paving the way for engaging in decentralized finance activities. DeFi represents a shift from traditional financial systems to an open, decentralized, and transparent digital ecosystem built on blockchain technology. At its core, DeFi leverages smart contracts on platforms like Ethereum to facilitate financial activities without relying on centralized intermediaries to hold their funds, such as banks or brokers.

Through DeFi, users can access a plethora of financial services, including lending, borrowing, trading, and yield farming, directly on the blockchain. This not only reduces costs and inefficiencies but also democratizes access. This ensures that financial products are available to a wider audience irrespective of geographic or economic barriers.

DeFi democratizes financial access, reduces fees from intermediaries, and promotes broader financial inclusion. DeFi allows us to go bankless: to leave Wall Street behind and thereby build DAOs that can change the world. So how do we use it?

Managing Risk

Before we continue, let's talk about managing risk.

Trading in DeFi, like any other form of investment, carries inherent risks, and effective risk management is crucial for safeguarding one's capital. One of the first steps in managing risk in the blockchain space is diversification. Instead of concentrating investments in a single cryptocurrency or project, traders can spread their capital across multiple assets. Diversification can mitigate potential losses if one or more investments perform poorly. Given the volatile nature of the cryptocurrency market, it's wise not to put all your eggs in one basket.

Another critical component of risk management is setting clear entry and exit points. On the flip side, setting take-profit points can ensure that profits are secured during moments of peak performance. Leveraging risk-management tools can help traders avoid making emotion-driven decisions, which often lead to significant losses, especially in the highly volatile environment of the blockchain world.

Last, staying informed is key. The blockchain and cryptocurrency space is rapidly evolving, with regulatory updates, technological advancements, and market-sentiment shifts happening continually. Being up-to-date with the latest news and trends can prepare traders for potential market shifts. Joining reputable cryptocurrency DAOs, following reliable news sources, and continually educating oneself can be beneficial. However, it's also essential to be wary of misinformation and misaligned incentives: the decentralized nature of blockchains can sometimes make them a breeding ground for unfounded rumors and hype. Beware any influencer who recommends an asset. Are they recommending it because it's truly got upside or because they've got a big bag of it?

Another way to manage risk when using DeFi is to look at the Lindy Effect of a system or token. The Lindy Effect is a concept proposing that the future life expectancy of nonperishable things like a technology or an idea is proportional to their current age. In other words, the longer something has been around, the longer it is likely to continue to be around. For example, a system that has been used ten million times for five years (like Ethereum) is likely to be in use for another five years, whereas a system that's been in use for only a day might not last. This principle can be applied to blockchains, smart contracts, wallets, or other things to help predict their longevity.

Most importantly, never invest more than you can afford to lose.

Swapping Currencies

At its core, a swap allows you to exchange one token for another. Popular centralized exchanges (CEXes for short) like Coinbase, Binance, and OKX facilitate this, but there are also decentralized exchange (DEXes for short) platforms such as Uniswap and Matcha. Swaps empower you to transform community currencies into stable assets like US dollar–denominated stablecoins or renowned cryptocurrencies like Bitcoin and Ethereum. Given their higher stability, stablecoins can provide a shield against market volatility, but be aware that even those can be risky. Smart-contract risk exists everywhere in DeFi, and it can wipe out large amounts of value.

Before diving in headfirst, it's imperative to examine the swap potential of the community currencies that you might have obtained from your journey through DAOs. Some currencies are nontransferable and cannot be swapped. For example, nontransferable tokens (NTTs) or soulbound tokens (SBTs) are bound to one wallet and carry information about the owner's identity and certification. Such currencies might serve solely as reputation currencies, and although they hold value, it's different from the financial value that's usually anticipated.

Another roadblock might be the absence of a trading pair for your token. A fresh token might lack a predefined pair, but given some time and growing popularity, enthusiasts might establish one to benefit from trading. Therefore, it's essential to inspect whether any trading pairs exist before opting in to earning those community currencies for your work.

QUEST 7: Swap currency or tokens.

To really understand how the world of DeFi works, you need to try it out. Take a token or community currency that you've earned during your journey through DAOs so far, and swap it for another so that you can see the wide range of what's available.

You can use a centralized exchange or a decentralized one.

As always, you can find detailed instructions at howtodao.xyz/quest.

Liquidity

Liquidity in the context of cryptocurrencies refers to the ease with which a community currency can be quickly bought or sold without causing a significant price change. High liquidity indicates a well-functioning market with many buyers and sellers, while low liquidity can lead to price volatility. Liquid markets are essential for traders and investors for efficient entry and exit points.

Liquidity can make or break your token-swapping endeavor. Acquiring a community token that is seemingly valued at a million dollars might seem enticing, but if there's insufficient liquidity, you might only retrieve a tiny fraction of its face value when attempting a swap. Using platforms like CoinGecko can offer insights into the token's liquidity, revealing available exchanges and the financial amount required to influence its price by 2 percent.

To give you an example, ETH to USDC—the second largest stablecoin representing the US dollar—is one of the most common swaps on the crypto market. Because of the size of the market and the deep liquidity, there won't be any price impact unless trades reach up into the millions of dollars; for example, the ETHUSD market needs to see more than $6 million worth of swaps to move the value of ETHUSD by 2 percent on the top exchanges. On the other hand, some "new coin" with a cute animal as a logo might need only a couple hundred dollars to move the price by many percentage points—the simple act of trading it could destroy its value. That's very low liquidity, and you might not be able to sell your community currency at all.

A token with substantial liquidity signifies easier trades and ensures price stability. Tokens traded on large centralized exchanges make them easier to trade, but this still does not guarantee deep liquidity.

Providing Liquidity

In order to ensure seamless token swaps, there must be sufficient liquidity. However, liquidity doesn't just appear out of thin air. Liquidity providers are responsible for introducing it. Take the decentralized exchange Uniswap as an example. When a trading pair is established between a community token and USDC, liquidity providers supply both assets, creating a liquidity pool for that specific trading pair. A liquidity pool is a reserve of multiple cryptocurrency tokens locked in a smart contract. To maintain balance in the trading pair and avoid one-way trading, the price movement adjusts based on supply and demand every time a trade is made. The depth of liquidity and the size of the trade determine how much the price will move. This price adjustment creates favorable pricing for the other side of the trade, which some traders may take advantage of by performing an opposite swap at a discounted price.

It's worth noting that the deeper the liquidity pool, the higher the price stability. As a result, you can swap a larger amount of your community currency for a stable price, and the value of your currency won't be drastically impacted. In the low-liquidity case, you might need to sell your community currency for a discounted price, which can vary from 1 percent to 99 percent. We call this "discount" a slippage, and it essentially occurs when a trade is at a different price than originally expected because of market fluctuation during the trade.

And these providers aren't fueled solely by the altruistic spirit of DeFi. They earn trading fees, which can range from 0.1 percent to 5 percent, democratizing the gains that, in a centralized world, would be monopolized by the exchange itself. You can also become a liquidity provider and earn some of those fees for yourself.

Lending

Having navigated the complexities of swaps and liquidity, it's time to delve deeper into another pillar of the DeFi universe: lending. At its core, lending in the decentralized domain mirrors traditional financial systems, albeit with a twist—there is no intermediary to trust with your funds. So lending in DeFi refers to the practice of lending assets, typically cryptocurrencies, through decentralized platforms or protocols without the need for traditional financial intermediaries like banks. Users can deposit their assets into these platforms, which then allow borrowers to take out loans against these deposits. Interest rates are often determined algorithmically based on supply-and-demand dynamics on the platform.

Borrowers usually have to provide collateral, often exceeding the amount they borrow, to secure their loans, reducing the risk for lenders. If a borrower's collateral value drops below a certain threshold because of market fluctuations, the platform may automatically liquidate a portion of the collateral to ensure that the loan remains overcollateralized, thus providing protection for lenders.

This financial dance isn't just an exchange of assets. It's underscored by an interest rate (APR) that the borrower pays for the privilege of the loan. The earned interest is channeled to those providing the liquidity, with a minor portion retained by the protocol facilitating the transaction.

If you are using DeFi to borrow, you will have to provide collateral to the lending smart contract. This collateral will secure the loan. You'll get it back when you repay the loan. If you are lending tokens, you will have to lock them in a smart contract, earning an APR on top.

Furthermore, for those with surplus stablecoins seeking returns on their holdings, lending protocols offer an avenue to high-yield savings accounts. By depositing their assets, they can earn interest, often outpacing traditional banking returns.

This is particularly important for DAOs, which can leverage lending to stake their community currency in exchange for USDC— allowing them to run and finance their business operations and expansions. If they find themselves with a surplus of funds, they can then use high-yield accounts to generate more revenue for the DAO.

QUEST 8: Provide liquidity for lending.

Once you've had the chance to familiarize yourself with liquidity—it's worth checking the liquidity of ETH as well as other coins in comparison—you can try to provide some liquidity for lending, earning a little extra coin for yourself in the process.

Go to app.aave.com, connect your wallet, and select what token you would like to supply to the platform to earn interest.

You can also take out a loan with your token as collateral.

As always, you can find detailed instructions at howtodao.xyz/quest.

Staking

One more way you can earn some yield is via staking.

Whereas mining was the primary way to earn rewards in the earlier days of blockchain, especially with Bitcoin and initially Ethereum, the landscape has shifted dramatically. Ethereum's transition from proof-of-work (PoW) to proof-of-stake (PoS) has changed the way users can earn rewards.

Under the PoW mechanism, participants used powerful hardware systems to solve complex computational puzzles. These miners, upon solving a puzzle, would confirm and validate transactions and, in return, earn a reward. But it was a resource-intensive process, requiring significant energy consumption, and it wasn't very climate friendly.

With PoS, on the other hand, the transaction validation process has evolved, and the energy consumption has been reduced by more than 99.9 percent. Instead of using computational power to validate transactions, validators stake a certain amount of their cryptocurrency as collateral. By staking, they essentially "bet" that they're confirming legitimate transactions. If they try to validate false transactions, they risk losing their staked assets. Usually a validator client like prysm will handle the correct transaction management. Hence, PoS offers a more energy-efficient mechanism, relying on financial incentives and disincentives to maintain network integrity.

Decentralized staking platforms pool staked assets from multiple participants and then use this pool to participate in the validation and consensus process. One noteworthy platform in this domain is Rocket Pool. It offers a decentralized solution, allowing users to stake their Ether and earn rewards without managing their own validators. Users contribute their Ether to a larger pool. When the pool earns validation rewards, contributors receive a share proportional to their stake. Rocket Pool handles the technical side, ensuring smooth operation in exchange, for a minimal deposit fee.

QUEST 9: Stake your ETH.

And the final step in becoming a DeFi expert: stake some ETH. Go to rocketpool.net, connect your wallet, click on "stake ETH," and follow the prompts.

In case you want to stake more than 8 ETH, you can run your own node through Rocket Pool's service and earn higher APR.

As always, you can find detailed instructions at howtodao.xyz/quest.

Evaluating Yield Sources

One thing to look at when evaluating staking or lending is where the yield comes from.

Understanding the sources of yield is essential for informed investment decisions. At its core, yield in DeFi represents the return on investment, but the origin and sustainability of this yield can vary significantly across platforms and protocols. When diving into DeFi yield opportunities, it's vital to differentiate between inflationary and noninflationary sources to assess the long-term viability and risks associated with the return.

Inflationary yield arises primarily from the issuance of new tokens as rewards for participation in a protocol, such as liquidity provision or staking. Although these rewards can initially offer enticingly high returns, they carry the risk of diluting the token supply. If the rate of new token issuance surpasses demand, the token's price could decline, potentially leading to diminishing returns for participants. The sustainability of such yields is often contingent on constant user growth and the hope that, over time, the protocol can transition to a more sustainable yield source or create token sinks that can counteract the inflationary pressures.

Noninflationary yield, meanwhile, is derived from actual economic activities within a DeFi protocol. Examples include trading fees on decentralized exchanges, interest from lending and borrowing activities, or any other revenue-generating actions within a platform. Since these returns aren't tied to the issuance of new tokens, they don't dilute the token supply and often represent more sustainable and genuine growth. However, the magnitude of these yields might be lower compared with inflationary yields, especially during early protocol stages. Investors should critically analyze the blend of inflationary versus noninflationary yields in any DeFi opportunity and consider the associated risks and the protocol's long-term economic model.

Managing Risk, Continued

Now that we've taken a tour of different things you can do in DeFi, let's revisit risk management. Risk management is key to making sure you don't lose your collateral in DeFi.

One way to manage risk is to check out the smart-contract audits being performed on your favorite protocols. Auditing is an integral part of the DeFi ecosystem. Renowned auditors collaborate with major protocols, ensuring that their smart contracts are secure. But while audits reduce the risk of vulnerabilities, they don't eliminate them entirely. Hence, platforms with a longer track record, like MakerDAO's core smart contracts, often exude more trust than newly minted ones.

A valuable resource to vet DeFi platforms is defillama.com. This site provides a comprehensive overview of various protocols and includes information on audits and their respective auditors. Always remember the adage "Do your own research." Familiarize yourself with a platform, its history, and community feedback before committing funds. In the world of DeFi, prudence isn't just advisable; it's essential.

CHAPTER SUMMARY:

How to Use Decentralized Finance

- After earning some tokens and taking your first steps into the world of DAOs, it's helpful to better understand the landscape of decentralized finance, or DeFi.

- Effective risk management is crucial for safeguarding one's capital. Strategies for managing risk include diversification, clear entry and exit points, staying informed, understanding the Lindy Effect, and never investing more than you can afford to lose.

- There are a number of different ways to participate in DeFi, including swapping currencies, providing liquidity, lending, yield farming, and staking.

- Always do your research and investigate any decentralized assets before you decide to participate in them.

9

HOW TO INVEST
WITH DAOs

O nce you've mastered how to get paid by DAOs and how to navigate the world of DeFi, you have the option to go even deeper. Increasingly, DAOs are providing remarkable investment opportunities that connect to the growing DeFI movement. Investing in a DAO typically involves purchasing tokens that represent membership or governance rights to a protocol, or within the DAO, but it can also mean direct financial investment in projects overseen by the DAO. As with DeFi, do your own research—this book is educational, not financial advice—and do not invest more than you can afford to lose.

Investment DAOs

In the crypto ecosystem, investment DAOs are emerging as democratic financial collectives wherein members collaboratively decide on investments, drawing parallels with traditional venture-capital dynamics but with a decentralized twist. A member's contribution isn't solely monetary; knowledge, research, and other skill sets are equally valuable.

These organizations often collaborate with early-stage companies, delving into a space where lengthy financial histories may not be available. Investment DAOs can be understood as decentralized collectives geared toward investments; they operate as pooled funds where members combine their resources, usually onchain, to support ventures aligned with the DAO's philosophy.

The distinction between investment DAOs and conventional funds lies in their operational mechanisms. In DAOs there's a heightened sense of collaboration. Members not only pool funds (often in the form of cryptocurrencies) but also contribute knowledge. This synergy can lead to investments being made through onchain transfers or even support-incubation models where the DAO might receive community currencies from the invested project. The structure of DAOs provides flexibility in how contributors are compensated and how investments are managed.

Investment DAOs offer each participant a stake in decision-making. This design ideally brings together both monetary and intellectual resources, paving the way for informed, collective decisions. It's not just about funds; it's also about gathering diverse knowledge to make the most astute investment choices.

However, DAOs aren't without challenges. These entities are still in nascent stages, so problems like under-participation or underuse of collective expertise are evident. Louder voices or central figures can emerge to ensure coordination and active participation, somewhat negating the decentralized ethos. To maximize the potential of DAOs, there's a need for cultural and operational shifts to make such decentralized participation more intuitive and natural for all members. In short, they're not perfect, but we know how to make them better, and we believe they'll get there.

A fascinating example in this realm is Hydra Ventures, which operates as a "fund of funds." Rather than simply being an investment DAO that chooses projects or start-ups to invest in, Hydra goes one step further by investing and incubating new investment DAOs: think of it as an accelerator for investment DAOs. The team at Hydra, led by Peter Pan, identifies individuals or groups with promising ideas for new investment DAOs, especially those targeting specific areas, be it geographical locations like Korea, ecosystems such as the urban space, or verticals like social.

In Hydra, if you're passive and not actively helping incubate the DAOs or making connections, you face the potential of dilution, meaning your investment might be worth less. Conversely, those actively contributing ideas or projects—or even participating in voting—stand to see their investment appreciated.

A standout feature of Hydra is its holistic approach to DAO incubation. It's not just about financials; Hydra extends its support far beyond. From assisting in establishing go-to-market strategies and identifying potential investors to pinpointing areas of focus, Hydra's backing is comprehensive. It guides you through legal, tax, operational frameworks, and accounting, ensuring that the incubated DAOs are compliant and optimally structured. This meticulous level of support helps nascent DAOs gain a deep understanding of frameworks, incentive models, and due diligence.

Launching an investment fund can be a daunting task, especially without the experience and pedigree of financial powerhouses like Goldman Sachs. However, investment DAOs offer an alternative solution. By partnering with robust entities like Hydra, these DAOs can access essential operational, compliance, and fundraising tools. Their potential success mostly depends on their profound domain-specific knowledge and influential connections within their chosen arena.

▌Spotting Opportunities

As a leader of Hydra, Peter Pan has become a key investor in the DAO ecosystem. But it wasn't always going to be that way. After Moloch-DAO, which strives to improve the Ethereum ecosystem and blockchain, launched on February 14, 2019, Peter attempted to join it. He was prepared to contribute time and money to something he thought represented the future of this crucial new way of organizing. He offered to put in 10 ETH—half of all the ETH he had back then. But he was rejected. He thinks he either wasn't cool enough or didn't have enough money. Instead, he was advised to fork MolochDAO—in other words, take the code that ran MolochDAO and redeploy it to center a separate but almost identical entity.

For Peter the result was MetaCartel, a fork of MolochDAO: a new DAO that would invest in the Ethereum ecosystem and fund user-focused projects with grants. Leveraging the innovative spirit of forking in the Web3 ecosystem, Peter tapped into a realm where open-source software doesn't just encourage, but practically necessitates, collaborative enhancement and expansion. Unlike traditional models, which often safeguard proprietary technologies, Web3 fosters a unique environment where technological developments are cumulative, communal efforts. Skillful developers, rather than being limited by the foundational stages of creation, can harness existing, openly accessible technology to build and innovate further. This approach not only drives forward an individual project but also enhances the overall evolution of the Web3 space, embodying a cooperative rather than a competitive spirit. It's a continuous, synergistic cycle where entities like MetaCartel not only benefit from prior advancements but also contribute back into the expansive, interconnected Web3 development environment, amplifying both their impact and the collective progression of the ecosystem.

Peter's route to becoming an investor in crypto ecosystems was unorthodox. He had no investing background, no track record. He had worked building online communities, so it felt natural operating crypto natively. And he learned quickly. He's also a pragmatist—he says he's someone with probably the least romantic views about the DAO space because he likes to think about it more from a practical point of view—as a means to structure organizations successfully.

Today, Peter's a partner in 1kx, an early-stage crypto investment firm that primarily invests in Web3. He champions the fact that DAOs can be set up onchain using smart contracts far, far quicker than traditional companies, and that the process is trustless: to trust Ethereum is much lower risk than trusting a bank you've never used before in a foreign country. "We're able to form organizations overnight very easily, and we will know the rules immediately based on those contracts, unlike starting a traditional company and signing up for a new bank account before which you need to read through pages and pages of paperwork," he says.

Peter also values the representation in a DAO community. It's not just the funders or the core team that built it—it's the participants and end users, too, through a better, more equitably distributed ownership model. Imagine if Uber was a DAO where drivers would be rewarded with stock that's inflating every quarter. Peter thinks you're likely going to find a better outcome for everyone: "One that rewards everyone far more fairly and cuts away like the passive middlemen. There's nothing bad about middlemen. It's just when they become purely passive and start to really hamstring the controls and extract value at a rate that they cannot really justify beyond the fact that they own the network."

Investment DAOs have become increasingly popular in recent times. But what attracts people to them? For many, it's the appeal of being a part of a decentralized investment system that promotes a flattened hierarchy and rewards meritocracy. Investment DAOs create an environment that encourages individuals to learn, contribute, and grow within the ecosystem, making them an ideal choice for those who seek such opportunities. The internet-native approach of DAOs also allows like-minded investors and enthusiasts to collaborate globally. In today's world, where traditional investment avenues are often out of reach for many, investment DAOs offer a gateway for those who wish to participate in decentralized investment.

In conclusion, while investment DAOs offer a unique and collaborative approach to investing, potential investors should be cautious, conduct extensive research, and seek legal advice to ensure the security of their investments.

Due Diligence

One of these methods of research is what's called "doing due diligence." We expect most organizations—most DAOs—to at least have "table stakes." Table stakes in a business deal typically refer to the minimum requirements or conditions that must be met for the deal to proceed or be considered viable, like ownership rights, governance structure, or costs involved. Peter Pan says that arguably there is less information available when thinking of investing in DAOs, despite their transparency. It can be hard to understand if there are any issues or problems because, like most companies, these are often discussed in back channels.

"Just like in a traditional Web2 company we might talk to employees as part of our due diligence, we often talk to DAO members or we look at the discourse, the discussions," Peter says. "We try to get insider feedback. But we would never get the full picture up front. I don't think it's necessarily a bad thing. I think it's the nature of how information works, but I think what is important is capital controls or protocol controls and protocol ownership and, most importantly, governance. Everyone thinks that it's just about having onchain controls, but none of that works or matters at all if you don't have effective off-chain governance that's coordinated effectively." In short: people still matter in DAOs.

Another risk is that the crypto ecosystem has different security models than the legacy financial system. Because of this, you need to be careful. What protects you in the old world does not protect you here. In the old financial system, you have an intermediary (a bank or government) that sits between you and your finances. In some parts of the world, these intermediaries work for you. In others, they extract from you or sometimes even steal from you. If you are privileged enough to live in a part of the world where banks or governments work for you and your community, congratulations! You can rely on your bank to give you access to your account if you get locked out, you can rely on investor protections to be assured that an influencer you follow is not pumping their bags when they promote an asset to you, and you can be assured that if someone steals your assets, you will have legal recourse against them.

In the crypto sphere, there are no such guarantees yet, although there are people who are hard at work trying to implement them. The crypto ecosystem is almost two decades old, whereas the legacy global financial system was largely built in the 1940s and 1950s, in the wake of World War II. It's what economists call "Bretton Woods"—the system of monetary management that established the rules for commercial relations among a total of forty-four countries, including the United States, Canada, Western European countries, and Australia, in 1944. The crypto sphere has had since 2009 to evolve, whereas the legacy system has evolved for nearly a century. Because of this, you must remember that "you are on the frontier." You can't rely on the same infrastructure that exists in a metropolis.

As with any disruptive force, the Internet of Finance faces its fair share of challenges. Skeptics argue that the dream of decentralized finance may give rise to a Wild West of financial chaos, leaving unsuspecting individuals vulnerable to fraud and exploitation. Striking the right balance between innovation and safeguarding the interests of the common good remains a paramount task for policymakers and technologists alike.

The worst thing in the world is to hear that someone has entered the world of DAOs only to find they've had their private keys and all their assets stolen because they entered them into a phishing app. Or they've followed some Ponzi scheme guy on Twitter pointing people to the next "hot" token. They bought it and then discovered that the influencer just dumped on them. It's important to tell people about the double-edged sword of crypto early on. Being pragmatic means learning to think adversarially and keeping your guard up. A lot of people lose their shirts in their first market cycle, but with prudent risk management many adverse outcomes can be avoided.

We can program our values into our money. Good values can create good money. Bad values can create bad money. There are profound implications in that. If we want to build a global community around funding open-source software because that's our value, that's great, but what if it's a big Ponzi scheme? What if you have just entered into a relationship with a low-level criminal out to scam you? Ethereum is a mirror that reflects ourselves and our values—and because of that, there are a lot of grifters out there who can ruin it. But the good news is you can avoid them with a bit of knowledge and skill. Crypto presumes a certain amount of agency and responsible decision-making from the user: to take custody of their own private keys and to not follow someone who doesn't have their best interests at heart because of the lack of the "nanny state" infrastructure. In the traditional financial system there are a lot of bumper rails to protect people from themselves, but those don't exist here.

On the digital frontier, a quiet revolution is unfolding. As we've witnessed the growth of DAOs, it's become apparent that they offer more than just financial freedom; they hold the promise of a world where transparency, equity, and cooperation stand at the forefront. They are the laboratories of democracy for the internet-native age, and as the curtain rises on this new era, the question is not whether DAOs will change the world but rather how fast and how profoundly they will usher in a future where power belongs to the many, not the few.

CHAPTER SUMMARY:
How to Invest with DAOs

- **FORKING FOR INNOVATION:** Forking in Web3 paves the way for cumulative tech progress, valuing collective advancements over proprietary stagnation.

- **HARMONIZING INVESTMENT METHODS:** Investing in DAOs requires blending blockchain's trustless verification with thorough due diligence.

- **CRYPTO'S UNIQUE SECURITY LANDSCAPE:** The crypto realm poses distinct security challenges, demanding caution and self-reliance from investors.

10

HOW TO USE DAOs TO JOIN SOCIAL CLUBS

Social DAOs are some of the most democratic DAOs out there these days. Their members and their missions are less focused on monetary gain and more on shared passions and community objectives. In essence, social DAOs are the heart and soul of the decentralized world, offering a warm and welcoming space for enthusiasts of varying interests and expertise. These are places where individuals can find kindred spirits, grow their knowledge, and collaborate on projects they're passionate about.

Take, for instance, BanklessDAO. Unlike many DAOs, which operate with the primary objective of financial growth or technological development, BanklessDAO is a community united by a shared mission. The doors are always open to anyone who aligns with the Bankless vision, and every member, from novice to expert, is a valued contributor—and there's always a more experienced member ready to guide you. The multiplicity of projects under its banner means everyone can find a niche that resonates with their passion.

While BanklessDAO is a testament to how vast and varied the tasks within a social DAO can be, it's not the only type. Some social DAOs have a lighter mood, focusing on activities just for fun. Others, like the Boys Club and SheFi, bridge the gap between social and impact. Their objective is to usher more women into the Web3 space. Offering educational programs and both virtual and real-world gatherings, they're not just about integration but also about building strong, supportive communities. For a woman eager to embark on a tech or Web3 journey, these DAOs are an invaluable starting point, providing mentorship, resources, and a sense of belonging.

For those dipping their toes into the vast ocean of Web3, joining a social DAO can be a gentle introduction. Whether your background is in finance, technology, or neither, these communities provide an excellent platform for exploration.

The beauty of social DAOs is that they mirror traditional community clubs. There's the same camaraderie, shared interests, and mutual respect, albeit on an internet-native platform—much like how you'd join a local soccer club, relishing the weekly matches and occasional postgame drinks. A social DAO is about coming together, usually not bound by stringent schedules, and partaking in shared activities. But in the case of DAOs, these activities might span different parts of the globe and deal with many issues.

In essence, social DAOs are about human connection in the decentralized world. They're spaces of collaboration, learning, and fun. And as the Web3 ecosystem continues to grow, so will the influence and reach of these social DAOs.

Art and Collectibles DAOs

With the rise of nonfungible tokens, there has been a surge in the shared ownership of digital assets. People from all over the world have been investing in new art, music, and other collectibles, forming groups united by their common passion. This has also been one of the reasons behind the growing interest in crypto and subsequently DAOs: some people may not be drawn to financial products and technical innovation, but they have a passion for art and collecting digital items, which led them to this new world. It's important to note that NFTs have a wide range of applications beyond just art and collectibles, but the connection between NFTs and DAOs in this context shows us their enormous potential. In this part of the book, whenever we refer to NFT DAOs, we are specifically talking about art and collectibles DAOs.

NFT communities are, at their essence, groups united by shared ownership of a particular collection. Buying into an NFT collection, whether it's a "Bored Ape" by Yuga Labs (you may recall the cartoon apes in hats and sunglasses that went viral) or a "World of Women," whose parent organization seeks to increase the number of women artists in the NFT space, automatically grants membership into its corresponding community. These communities are verified by platforms like Collab. Land and represent people who have a vested interest in a shared asset. Naturally, there's an intrinsic desire to see the value of this shared asset appreciate, so it creates a collective effort toward a common goal.

Anjali, the founder of Collab.Land, introduced a novel concept termed "transaction to trust." Unlike conventional dynamics in finance or business where trust is established before any transaction takes place, within the NFT ecosystem the act of purchasing a shared asset initiates early trust among members. The mutual ownership of an asset, such as an NFT, becomes the foundational pillar of trust, catalyzing collaboration and communal efforts from the outset.

As NFT communities matured, elements of governance began to emerge with the common goal of growing the asset value. They began operating with structures that echoed traditional DAOs, making decisions on various topics such as marketing, partnerships, or project enhancements.

NFT communities can be classified into three types. The first type governs a specific collection of NFTs or a particular artist, such as

CryptoPunks (often credited for starting the NFT craze in 2021) or Beeple (aka Mike Winkelmann, considered a pioneer of NFT art). Members of these communities work together to support the growth of the collection. This type is the most common NFT DAO.

The second type creates a decentralized art-curator system that governs multiple pieces of art from different collections. The "whale community" is an example of this type; crypto "whales" are people or entities that possess large amounts of cryptocurrency. Members of this community possess an ERC-20 token called the "whale token," which grants them exclusive club membership, voting rights, and curatorial privileges over the NFT vault.

The third type supports the creation of art within a particular style or brand. To simplify things, let's use music enthusiasts as an analogy. Just like music fans, NFT community members can be divided into three groups. Some are devoted to a single artist, while others are united by their shared role in the music community, while still others appreciate a variety of music.

Nouns DAO offers a unique and impactful approach to integrating NFTs and DAOs. Owning an NFT isn't just about digital ownership; it's your ticket to the DAO. With more than eight hundred Nouns NFTs, not one is currently up for sale on the market. The DAO, true to its essence, mints, or creates, a single NFT daily, and that's forever. If you're keen on joining the DAO, you need to seize the day because acquiring that NFT on its minting day is the only way to gain membership. This "one NFT a day" policy ensures scarcity and demand, making Nouns a unique and exclusive community to be a part of.

Although getting into the community may not be easy, the possibilities and opportunities are significant once you're in. By owning a single NFT, members can propose ideas that directly impact the community's direction. This is not just an idealistic community, but also one with considerable assets. The Nouns Collective has successfully gathered more than 15,000 ETH—about $31 million USD—from its members by issuing daily NFTs. These funds are strategically used based on proposals that enhance the Nouns ecosystem. The community is also becoming more decentralized, with many sub-DAOs or even forks of the original collection popping up to support various unique areas, ranging from fun events to developing solutions or supporting the public good.

What sets Nouns apart is that although it isn't curating art directly, it plays a pivotal role in supporting art creation under the Nouns brand. Artists can receive funding to craft novel "nounish" art—colorful, 32×32 pixel avatars with hundreds of combinations of accessories— amplifying the brand's aesthetic and fostering creativity. This synergy between nurturing artistry and bolstering the brand's identity has enabled Nouns to create a thriving community where art and governance converge.

QUEST 10: Explore an NFT collection.

You can explore various NFTs on Rarible.com or Opensea .io. One of the prominent communities is worldofwomen .art, which champions Web3 inclusivity. On its website, you can delve into its mission and its collective objectives.

If you wish to become an active participant in this community, you need to purchase its NFT. However, to complete the quest, it's sufficient to explore the community to grasp its essence beyond mere speculation.

As always, you can find detailed instructions at howtodao.xyz/quest.

ConstitutionDAO

One of the most exciting recent examples of both an art and collectibles DAO and a social DAO, with a little bit of impact DAO mixed in, was ConstitutionDAO. In November 2021, over the course of five days, an online collective calling itself ConstitutionDAO managed to crowdfund $47 million worth of the cryptocurrency Ether. Its objective was to purchase an original copy of the United States Constitution. In order to participate, members exchanged their cryptocurrency for tokens that represented voting power as they united to acquire a tangible symbol of democracy, and these members could then vote on what to do with this copy of the Constitution.

Unfortunately, despite raising an astonishing amount of crypto, ConstitutionDAO was eventually outbid by a billionaire hedge-fund investor called Ken Griffin. Throughout the auction, the two sides engaged in a gradual escalation, incrementally raising their bid by a million dollars each time. Ultimately, though, as the gavel was about to drop, ConstitutionDAO conceded defeat, informing its backers that if it continued it wouldn't have enough money needed to insure, store, and transport the document. Griffin, meanwhile, ended up parting with $43 million to purchase his copy.

Although it was Griffin who ended up with the grand prize, the exercise was far from a failure; what ConstitutionDAO had done was prove that its unique vision of a democratic, borderless, and decentralized community pooling its resources to achieve big, important things was indeed possible. It was a novel approach to civic engagement, reimagining a democratic process that typically happens within the chambers of legislatures, town halls, or boardrooms, transplanting it into an internet-native landscape. Its founders called it "a beautiful experiment in a single-purpose DAO."

ConstitutionDAO dared to ask: can collective decision-making thrive without intermediaries, relying on code and consensus mechanisms instead of elected representatives? The blockchain, touted for its transparency and security, shone a light on ConstitutionDAO's inner workings—the decisions, strategies, and conflicts all remained under the scrutinizing gaze of the people. The sheer audacity of a group of individuals, connected solely through digital networks, striving to acquire a historical document that embodied the principles of governance and justice galvanized conversations about the evolving nature of democracy.

QUEST 11: Join a club.

Life is not just about work: join a social DAO with like-minded people and learn about their mission, as well as how you can be part of it.

Some examples include Kraus House, FWB, BanklessDAO, and SheFi, but there are many more: you can check our website for a more comprehensive list.

As always, you can find detailed instructions at howtodao.xyz/quest.

CHAPTER SUMMARY:
How to Use DAOs to Manage Club Membership

- DAOs aren't just for work: there are DAOs for art, DAOs that are like social clubs, and DAOs that are coming together over unique missions and shared interests.

- NFT communities can be classified into three types: specific collections, a decentralized art-curator system that governs multiple pieces of art from different collections, and the creation of art within a particular style or brand.

- Examples of DAOs that function like clubs include Nouns DAO, BanklessDAO, and ConstitutionDAO.

- If you can do it in the physical world, chances are there's a DAO for it, too.

Part Three

Achieving
DAO Mastery

11

WHY (AND HOW) GITCOIN BECAME A DAO

The inception of Gitcoin can be traced back to a profound understanding of the value of open-source software. Before the boom of open source in the 2000s, software companies monopolized their innovations. Open-source software disrupted this dominance, enabling innovation and community-driven growth. By 2009, the estimated combined value of global open-source software was nearly $400 billion.

Recognizing the potential in this space, Gitcoin aimed to bridge the gap between open-source developers and those requiring their services. It sought to eliminate the need for recruiters, providing a platform where open-source developers could connect directly with potential employers in a crypto-native environment.

The initial version of Gitcoin, developed in 2017, was a platform that primarily focused on "bounties," which are essentially tasks with specified rewards, as explained in Chapter Seven. Pivoting from this idea, Gitcoin began focusing on "virtual hackathons," which was a more widely understood concept in the developer community. The Gitcoin team continued experimenting with various features throughout its evolution, focusing on the most successful ones; one of these was Gitcoin Grants, a Web3 crowdfunding platform a bit like Kickstarter.

Gitcoin Grants, which launched in 2019, would resonate with many people because of its unique approach to promoting and supporting worthy projects. Instead of relying on the conventional funding methods that significant stakeholders could easily sway, Gitcoin Grants would embrace the ethos of quadratic funding, a concept pioneered by Ethereum's cofounder Vitalik Buterin. This innovative method revolutionized how projects were financed by ensuring that every contribution, regardless of size, played a significant role in determining the project's success.

Quadratic funding is a way of running democratic financial-matching campaigns—and it seemed like the perfect solution for Gitcoin Grants. Quadratic funding allocates a pool of matching funds according to an algorithm that says the number of contributors matters more than the amount funded. In other words, numerous micro-donations beat out the same amount from fewer larger donors. This model values many people believing in the project rather than one or two individuals; it's democratically financed by a lot of people who love the idea, rather than one or two people who have a vested interest in it succeeding. If you raised $10 from each of ten contributors for $100 total, for example, and someone else raised $100 from a single contributor, with quadratic funding you'd get much more of the matching pool because you had a broader base of support. This mechanism gets people off their butts to vote because even a $1 contribution can make a big difference in allocation of the matching pool.

This mechanism is also very democratic: it pushes power to the edges, away from so-called "whales"—individuals or companies with large cryptocurrency accounts that could influence the market and price fluctuations—as well as other central power brokers. When a project gets popular enough, the funding mechanism reinforces the incentive structure of quadratic funding as a fundamentally democratic institution. Gitcoin Grants evolved to be the largest quadratic funding experiment in existence, eventually causing Buterin to call

it a significant pillar of the Ethereum ecosystem in April 2020—
something that did much to elevate Gitcoin's status among hard-core
crypto nerds.

Gitcoin Grants would amplify the voices of the many over the few.
The traction that Gitcoin Grants could achieve would further cement
Gitcoin's reputation and importance within the crypto community.

We launched Gitcoin Grants in Q1 2019. By 2020, it was beginning
to really heat up, and we hit our first crowdfunding round with more
than $1 million the following year. Between 2019 and 2024, Gitcoin
was able to fund $60 million worth of public goods through more than
4 million unique donations.

During its growth phase, Gitcoin broadened its focus from exclusively supporting open-source software to embracing a wider range
of digital public goods, including education and information. These
kinds of public goods are vital to society yet challenging to monetize.
By nature, they are nonexcludable, ensuring that everyone has access
without restrictions, and nonrivalrous, meaning that one person's
consumption doesn't prevent another's. This inherent accessibility
contrasts with traditional business models, which often depend on
excludability to charge users for access or consumption.

Gitcoin Grants felt like a natural fit. It was about supporting good
projects and donating to them because you wanted to see them continue. The crypto economy goes through cycles of bullishness and
bearishness. Between 2018 and 2020 there was a bear market in which
we saw a prolonged drop in investment prices and investors clinging
to their portfolios with anxiety and desperation. During this time,
capital was scarce. Many projects relied on Gitcoin partially or fully
for financial support. It was hard to get funding elsewhere, and venture capitalists weren't running around with an open checkbook. In
2020 Gitcoin was allocating between $3 million and $6 million per

quarter to some of the best projects in the ecosystem, making it one of the more significant funders in the space for projects that weren't good at writing grant applications or raising money.

But we were facing the same challenges as other projects. Software development isn't cheap, and we were burning a lot of money. We had some revenue, but not enough to cover our expenses. With staying alive being our primary focus, things were getting stressful. We had to maintain our hackathon and nonprofit Grants business lines on a small quarterly budget. Gitcoin's staff was burned out. Resources were thin. Gitcoin was now a darling of the Ethereum ecosystem, but, in truth, it wasn't making much money. Joe Lubin, the founder of Consensys, which invested in Gitcoin in 2017, never wavered in his belief in the company, but we couldn't rely on Joe's benevolence toward us forever. And we couldn't pay our bills with the social capital generated from funding so many other projects.

We had another challenge that compounded the above problems: we realized that if Gitcoin Grants was going to be a core pillar of a decentralized ecosystem, it couldn't be centralized. If it was a company, it wouldn't be credibly neutral, democratic, or community driven. We knew we didn't want to go down that road of centralization, but we weren't sure which direction to go. In the beginning we wanted Gitcoin to become a platform cooperative or a collectively owned business—but how would we do that? There was no How to DAO playbook.

Prior to 2020, there weren't a lot of DAO initiatives that had achieved notable success, but there were a few high-profile failures, like The DAO. However, the summer of 2020, known as DeFi Summer, marked a resurgence of DAOs. That year also saw the growth of some highly respected DAO projects, such as the funding club MolochDAO, Yearn.Finance, and Uniswap, a decentralized exchange. MakerDAO, the creators of the stablecoin $DAI, was also gaining traction. The common denominator among these projects was their governance by DAOs, which contributed to their remarkable success.

Should Gitcoin become a DAO? Could this be the way that we might realize our goal of going off the beaten start-up path toward something more aligned, like a platform cooperative? (A platform cooperative is a cooperatively owned business that uses a website, mobile app, or protocol to sell whatever its goods or services are.) Gitcoin had grown to a point of somewhat systemic importance in the Ethereum ecosystem. Was it now time to forge its path forward as a DAO?

In the beginning, our flirtation with DAOs was merely casual. But the more we opened our minds to the possibilities, the more our conviction grew. One of the data points that pushed us further in that direction was a blog post by Buterin that outlined the difference between traditional organizations and decentralized autonomous organizations. Buterin said DAOs were good . . .

1. . . . at creating democratic decision-making environments.
2. . . . at being resistant to hacks from powerful attackers or censorship from the state.
3. . . . when credible fairness (predictability, neutrality, and nondiscrimination) is important.

We had read the tea leaves, and we knew that if we were going to build critical infrastructure for funding public goods, we needed to check all three of these boxes. We would fulfill our original aspirations of becoming a platform cooperative, but we would do this by pursuing the DAO path. So by autumn 2020, it was time to make Gitcoin a DAO. The project I started three years earlier would go through its next evolution—to become decentralized.

Have you ever had one of those moments that are so surreal you wonder, "How did we get here?" When Buterin wrote about Gitcoin during its growth spurt in 2019 and 2020, we felt that this was our "how we got here" moment: the alpha nerd of the Web3 ecosystem was telling us the app we'd designed could be crucial. But it was bittersweet because we realized that Gitcoin, the company, was fundamentally misconfigured if we wanted to make it a larger success.

So we tipped over the apple cart and began the long journey to turn Gitcoin into a DAO.

It would be a long road, and we couldn't do it overnight. We'd need to rewrite Gitcoin's legal, governance, product, finance, and technology layers—a path known in the crypto space as "progressive decentralization." Instead of swallowing an elephant, we would decentralize in small chunks over time. The start of this would be to bootstrap DAO decision-making—or governance. For me, this meant it was time to move on from being ultimately responsible for all the decisions for the corporation to becoming one of many good stewards of a decentralized network instead. Eventually, that would mean leaving its governance entirely in the hands of Gitcoin's contributors and community. Other than studying previous DAO launches, there was no real playbook for any of this. We were on the frontier.

In May 2021, we launched Gitcoin DAO. Through the new governance process (which you can read at manual.gitcoin.co), community members could submit proposals that would then be voted on; then the DAO could allocate capital to various initiatives. One of the most essential proposals was a rewrite of the Gitcoin Grants platform, to be decentralized and modular. We really wanted to achieve that attribute that Vitalik talks a lot about, a value known as "credible neutrality," which is a mechanism for nondiscrimination, treating everyone fairly. How do you know that the service provider is neutral to everything that it serves? How do you, as a user of Gitcoin, know that the CEO is not behind the scenes, turning the dials toward his favorite projects? The answer is you implement a protocol that, once on the blockchain, embedded in a smart contract, cannot be tampered with. This gets at the heart of what blockchains are and what they're for.

Another key benefit of the DAO-based architecture is modularity—the degree to which a system's components may be separated and re-combined, sometimes with the benefit of flexibility and variety in use. When Gitcoin Grants was rebuilt to be modular, anyone could then download the software, substitute out a component for one they thought worked better, and then deploy the software for their own use. Modularity is a powerful way of enabling freedom of choice for communities of web applications. The market will decide which mechanisms will succeed, not a central team.

Back when Gitcoin was centralized, we developed a tool that enabled people to donate, and we had the ability to update the production version of it. Unfortunately, this model posed the same transparency and trust problems that many of the pillars of Web2 suffer from.

Blockchains allowed us to move from socialware (mechanisms that create assurances through human relationships, incurring a high social-coordination cost) to trustware (mechanisms that create assurances through technology, incurring a low social-coordination cost). With so-cialware, your trust in security is placed in the hands of another person, like a bank teller; with trustware, trust is with technology or a machine, like a vending machine. When Gitcoin was a company, it was based on socialware only. You had to trust that the people behind the company were acting in your best interests. Once Gitcoin had become a DAO and Gitcoin Grants had become a protocol, you could now be sure that it was implemented correctly because it was governed by trustware.

Another thing we wanted to avoid was becoming an extractive

corporation that needed to answer only to its investors. Instead, we wanted to do what was good for the ecosystem as a whole. It turns out this idea has a deeply rooted history in political philosophy. It's called "consent of the governed," and it refers to the notion that a government's legitimacy and moral right to use state power are justified and lawful only when given consent by the people over whom that political power is exercised (as opposed to the government's legitimacy coming from the "divine right of kings," as it had in the feudal ages).

Web2 companies did not have the consent of the governed. We are all digital serfs in Twitter's or Facebook's land insofar as when we post content to those platforms, we don't truly have any rights over this content. We didn't want that for Gitcoin. What if Gitcoin could close the "consent of the governed" loop between those with political power and those upon which that power was exercised? When Gitcoin became a DAO, it would go from having a board of directors, which hired and fired the CEO (Kevin), to letting its members participate in decision-making through a voting process, giving them a greater say in the future direction of the platform. This was the goal when we created GTC—Gitcoin's governance token. We would issue all of the contributing members this native token that token holders would then use to cast votes and govern. Gitcoin Grants would essentially become a democratically run organization controlled by its members. From the moment of the DAO launch, GTC holders could vote in order to make decisions about budgets and approve work streams.

One of the core constraints with governance tokens is the amount of governance apathy that exists in internet-native communities. People don't have the muscle to govern their communities, and many users don't know how or where to vote, which frequently requires them to use other platforms, such as Snapshot or Tally, in order to participate. This friction in researching your choices and then voting has resulted in low participation: most of the popular DAOs in 2021 saw only 1 percent to 10 percent voter turnout. So the next step in designing our DAO was to think about how we could increase participation.

We attempted to solve this with a feature called vote delegation. The GTC token launch enabled token holders to delegate their votes to individuals who shared their values and were willing to participate actively in Gitcoin governance on their behalf. In the beginning, there were eighteen thousand token holders, and most of those delegated their voting rights to forty or fifty people called stewards—because henceforth they would be stewarding the protocol. The stewards signed up on our governance forum and were usually (1) passionate Gitcoin users, (2) Ethereum community members, or (3) Gitcoin team members. They would manage their constituencies, who could change their delegation at any time to another delegate if they felt that they were not aligned with that particular steward anymore. This is a mechanism called liquid democracy: a form of delegation democracy where an electorate engages in collective decision-making through direct participation and dynamic representation.

By turning Gitcoin into a DAO, we'd created a positive feedback loop where the community of people who had used (or were currently using) our products were now the ones governing those same products. It was really about fully transferring the control of every layer of what I call the decentralization layer cake to the community—legal, governance, product, finance, and technology. In keeping with the philosophy of progressive decentralization, this was an iterative process.

Upon the DAO launch, 50 percent of the GTC tokens that were minted went into the community treasury and 50 percent to people who had helped Gitcoin in the past, which included users, team members, and investors. It was quite profound that 50 percent of governance rights were going to people who helped usher Gitcoin to where it was when we launched it as a DAO and 50 percent would go to those in its DAO-based future. This was our karmic handshake with the universe: we got it this far, now we were giving it away, and the community could take it from here.

Decentralizing control and decentralizing accountability are everything in a DAO, and maximizing transparency in decision-making is crucial to ensuring that everyone has the same level of information. Within a DAO, you can see the top voters in the community, the different proposals coming into the governance forum, and the assets in the treasury. Decisions on the distribution of resources and the prioritization of work are made in written budget requests; it begins with the particular work stream preparing a plan, including resourcing and milestones for the next time period, and submitting it on the DAO's public forum. Once a proposal attracts enough discourse on the platform and all major comments have been incorporated, it goes to an onchain vote where community stewards use tokens to vote on whether they want the proposal to pass. If it passes, tokens are released from the treasury into the workstream, and that project can begin.

Through the course of a couple of years, Gitcoin Grants had gone from a company that was centralized to one in which decisions have begun to be made in public through consensus among the delegates of the token holders.

In parallel with this evolution, the Allo Protocol was born. (*Allo* is short for *capital allocation*.) Originating as the foundation of Gitcoin's quadratic funding rounds, it has metamorphosed into an open-source protocol, offering communities an expansive palette of fund-allocation mechanisms tailored to their unique goals. By using the Allo Protocol, DAOs can take the capital-allocation mechanisms behind Gitcoin Grants and integrate them into their own tools.

Gitcoin Grants has evolved since its inception in 2019 from exclusively supporting open-source software to championing causes like climate, Ethereum infrastructure, and privacy. Now, as a decentralized solution bolstered by the Allo Protocol, this versatile tool facilitates seamless management of grant programs, catering to any community and encompassing all possible causes.

This was all highlighted by the most profound moment: Gitcoin as a community-governed organization decided to change its overall mission statement. When Kevin was CEO, he established Gitcoin's mission to "build and fund public goods," and it served us well during those years. The DAO, led by contributor Laura Banks, decided collectively that Gitcoin would adjust its mission statement, stating, in plain English, what it did: "Fund what matters." And it is beautiful because it's much more relatable and intuitive. The DAO conceived a more concise and relatable expression of the mission than any individual could ever have.

Gitcoin's journey of progressive decentralization started on May 25, 2021, with the launch of GTC. But it continues to this day.

QUEST 12: Participate in the governance of a DAO.

Want to get a better feel for Gitcoin's journey and why being a DAO is the perfect format for us? Sign up to the Gitcoin Forum at gov.gitcoin.co and then read a few posts. Whether you express your opinion through a detailed comment or simply show appreciation with a Like, your engagement makes Gitcoin what it is.

All information about gitcoin can be found at howtodao.xyz/gitcoin.

As always, you can find detailed instructions at howtodao.xyz/quest.

CHAPTER SUMMARY:

Why (and How) Gitcoin Became a DAO

- **GITCOIN'S EVOLUTION:** Initially a centralized company, Gitcoin transitioned into a decentralized platform through Ethereum, ensuring transparent and democratic decision-making. This transformation was epitomized by the DAO's collective decision to refine Gitcoin's mission statement to "fund what matters," reflecting a more intuitive and relatable goal.

- **FINANCIAL AND OPERATIONAL ADVANCEMENTS:** Gitcoin diversified its revenue streams, moving beyond optional donation fees to assist other DAOs in deploying their treasuries, thereby ensuring financial sustainability. Significant innovations like the Public Goods Network (PGN) and the Allo Protocol were introduced, reinforcing Gitcoin's commitment to funding public goods and providing communities with flexible fund-allocation mechanisms.

- **THE POTENTIAL AND CHALLENGES OF DAOS:** Embodying the promise of Web3, DAOs like Gitcoin represent a shift toward democratized engagement, offering a solution to the centralization issues prevalent in Web2. However, the path involves various challenges and setbacks, necessitating a balance between optimism and realism in acknowledging both the successes and the inevitable failed experiments in the quest for decentralized progress.

12

WHY START A DAO?

Starting a DAO can be as easy as creating a multisignature wallet (a wallet that requires two or more wallets to agree to sign a transaction) that you and a friend share. And it can be as complicated as launching a venture-scale start-up. This chapter will explore the possibilities of starting a DAO, ranging from the simplistic to DAOs with world-changing potential.

Embarking on creating a DAO is reminiscent of pioneering a start-up or nurturing a community in the conventional world. The foundational elements—mission, purpose, and culture—remain intact. However, where traditional entities often face boundaries and scale limitations, DAOs replicate these setups and amplify them, unlocking global reach and borderless operations from day one.

As you work on building and growing a DAO, keep in mind that the progress is not a straight path. Sometimes it's a case of one step forward, two steps back. Success comes from taking an iterative and agile approach, especially when dealing with unpredictable factors such as the crypto market or herd behavior. This iterative approach involves the observe-orient-decide-act-learn-repeat loop, which should be incorporated into every phase of your DAO's development. By holding on to this mindset—envisioning a DAO as an evolutionary organization and continuously iterating through this adaptive cycle—

you're poised to harness the best of the internet-native world, ensuring resilience, adaptability, and growth.

A DAO's success is mostly determined by its foundational principles, its members, and the guiding rules of operation. When creating a DAO, whether in blockchain or traditional business, a comprehensive approach is necessary. The goal is to create an entity with a vision, strategy, and pulse beyond its structural facade.

Start with Your Mission

Embarking on the journey to create a DAO necessitates more than technological savvy; it demands a harmonizing mission, innovative technology, and strategic planning. The first question any creator must ask themselves is "Why should this DAO exist?" The existence of your DAO should hinge upon identifying a concrete, prevalent problem in society or within a particular niche that has yet to be optimally addressed or solved. This identified issue doesn't just act as a starting point but also serves as an ongoing reference to ensure that the DAO's endeavors remain relevant and purposeful.

Moving forward, developing a solution that does more than just better the current standard is crucial. It should signify a considerable advancement in existing capabilities, ensuring that the DAO doesn't just introduce a new solution but is superior and impactful. Your DAO's technological aspect must seamlessly intertwine with its mission, ensuring a symbiotic relationship where one consistently complements and enhances the other.

In addition to technology, infusing your DAO with a unique insight into the identified problem and momentum toward its viable solutions is paramount. This unique perspective ensures that the pathway carved out by your DAO is new, unsaturated, and thus likely to encounter reduced competition. In the internet-native space, where echoes are many, your DAO should be a distinctive voice that brings fresh perspectives and solutions into light and does not just replicate existing systems.

Subsequently, strategy comes into play. A strategy birthed from robust market research and understanding should target the ideal demographic and navigate through the potential collaborators or competitors. It's crucial to remember that strategy is dynamic, ever-adapting, and continuously realigning following ongoing insights and ever-changing landscapes.

As the DAO comes into existence, making sure that its journey is adaptive and inclusive is crucial. The DAO must be fluid, evolving in tandem with technological advancements, market trends, and societal needs, ensuring its sustained relevance and impact. In essence, crafting a DAO involves a meticulous weaving of mission, technology, and strategy where each element is aligned and interlaced, enabling your DAO to stand as a beacon of tangible change and innovation.

Build an Economic System

DAOs benefit from the flexibility to either develop their own economic models or integrate into larger ecosystems, such as Ethereum with ETH or the United States with USDC, broadening their potential for impact and longevity. Establishing a solid economic foundation is crucial for a DAO's success. By thoroughly understanding the industry it will operate in, clarifying its main objective, and conducting in-depth market research, a DAO can position itself as a competitive leader and uniquely carve out its niche in the market. Furthermore, a well-designed economic model is essential not only for funding operations but also for incentivizing actions that align with the DAO's goals. This strategic approach ensures the sustainability and effectiveness of the DAO in achieving its objectives, whether it operates as a for-profit, a nonprofit, or a social club.

One pivotal pitfall to sidestep is perceiving a token launch as a business plan. Tokens can be potent tools in a DAO's arsenal, but they should not become the sole focus. Let's draw wisdom from DAOs like Optimism. Instead of hastily diving into a token launch, it carefully crafted a technology that addressed a genuine need in Ethereum, sculpting a community and proving the technology's value. The subsequent token launch was not a desperate plea for relevance but a calculated stride, driven by proven value and community support, ensuring that it was successful and synergistic with Optimism's preexisting values and community.

Your DAO should function like an institution, where the token is not the foundation but rather a building block, woven together with other essential elements such as technology, community, and genuine value. By doing so, you can not only ensure the continued existence of your DAO but also allow it to thrive and create a lasting impact.

Assemble a Team

Constructing a team for your DAO venture is about more than just forming an alliance. It's a lively adventure that requires passion, unity, and adaptability. In the vast and boundless domains of DAOs, it's crucial to build an ensemble where each member contributes to a harmonious melody of a unified vision and purpose.

Envision your initial team not merely as collaborators but as a close-knit family of pioneers, each member carrying a flame ignited by the "why" that propels your DAO's journey. The team you have is the backbone of your organizational culture. It brings your values and mission to life and makes them a reality. This team does more than just have the necessary skills—it is the essence of your DAO.

It is also worthwhile to study projects where shared values and culture are weak, and where ventures struggle to coordinate diverse and vast amounts of contributors. These downside scenarios reveal the shaky journeys of projects that sought to scale prematurely through tactics like extensive NFT drops.

Incorporate this idea into your narrative: a great team goes beyond simply being competent. It resonates throughout the organization with passionate alignment with your vision and the capability to steer your DAO toward the horizons of realization. Your team should be a vibrant entity, able to adapt to any challenge and approach every opportunity with a unified purpose. This ensures that the melody your team creates resonates, endures, and stands strong.

Case Studies

Three examples of DAOs that successfully defined their mission and took concrete steps toward achieving their goal are ConstitutionDAO, Nouns DAO, and MakerDAO. The first provides an example of a DAO meant to achieve a short-term goal, and the other two are instances of DAOs designed to foster a long-term community.

As outlined earlier in this book, ConstitutionDAO had a very clear goal: buy an original copy of the Constitution. The DAO gathered people and money dedicated to this effort, and then made an attempt to buy the copy when it was put up for auction. While the effort ended up being unsuccessful, it came very close, and ConstitutionDAO illustrates how effective DAOs can be at achieving this sort of short-term goal.

Nouns DAO's initial mission was to promote the Nouns brand. To do this, it decided to launch one NFT per day that would enable new contributors to participate in governance, enabling users to be involved in the community for the long term rather than just raising funds from one-offs.

MakerDAO, on the other hand, aimed to enable the generation of DAI, an unbiased currency and decentralized stablecoin. In order to do this, the DAO generated yield from the issuance of DAI that could then be channeled into further funding the ecosystem's development and creating stability.

For both Nouns DAO and MakerDAO, these initial steps kept people involved and helped to facilitate continued growth and ongoing investment.

CHAPTER SUMMARY:
Why Start a DAO?

- Starting a DAO can be easy or complicated, depending on the ultimate goals of the DAO.

- When you start your DAO, it's essential to have a mission that will help guide you as you build and evolve.

- You also need an economic model that can help you stand out in your marketplace and avoid leaning on a token launch as your only means of making money.

- A good team will be at the heart of your DAO, and building that team is a crucial step toward success.

13

HOW TO BUILD A DAO

N ow that you've figured out why you want to start a DAO, let's investigate how to do it on a more technical level. Let's start with the simplest DAO example possible: a group chat with a shared bank account.

Imagine you're forming a group for annual vacations or for a shared interest like maintaining a tennis club. Historically, you'd rely on centralized trust systems: a single joint bank account or a physical cashbox. These methods, while simple, place enormous trust in individuals, often creating bottlenecks or potential points of failure.

Now transpose this scenario to a digital environment, where relationships aren't forged over generations but over shared interests and online interactions. Trust here becomes fragile, and conventional methods prove inadequate. The solution? Multisignature accounts on the blockchain. It's akin to having a joint bank account with a built-in consensus mechanism. If the group comprises five, you can set a threshold—maybe three are needed to approve a transaction. It democratizes the process, dilutes power concentration, and, in essence, becomes a simple yet powerful representation of what DAOs promise: decentralized decision-making.

So if you are thinking of creating an online community with shared resources, multisig is the only thing you need now.

QUEST 13: Create a multisig wallet.

Now that you've spent some time participating in DAOs, the next step in your journey is to start your own. Find a friend or colleague, and start a multisig together to pool resources for a new project. If you can't find a friend or colleague, you can use two wallets you own.

To create a multisig, go to Safe.global, click "create a wallet," and follow the prompts.

As always, you can find detailed instructions at howtodao.xyz/quest.

The multisig is merely an introduction to DAOs—a foundation, if you will. When you need to evolve from the rudimentary "one person, one vote" system and venture into intricate governance structures, tools like DAOHaus and Aragon enter the picture.

The design space here is vast. Any smart-contract–based tool that coordinates human behavior can be thought of as a DAO. A tool like Gitcoin Grants can be thought of as an ephemeral DAO creator—a Gitcoin Grants round is a DAO that lasts for only two weeks while the crowdfunding campaign is happening.

Although the joint account remains a cornerstone of DAO creation, platforms like DAOHaus, Aragon, Moloch, and Gitcoin Grants amplify the possibilities. Think about layering complementary governance mechanisms together. For example, MolochDAO allows people to pool their resources and collaborate more effectively on funding and executing projects, operating on the Ethereum blockchain and allowing members to collectively allocate funds for projects voted on by the community. By simplifying smart contracts, it creates less chance that they could be exploited; the more complicated your smart contract is, the more attack surface area there is. Through this innovation, Moloch helped address many of the concerns that still existed around DAOs after the original hack of The DAO.

So how does this all work? Imagine this scenario: Person A contributes ten hours' worth of work monthly to a project, while Person B dedicates forty hours' worth weekly. It's clear that Person B's stake and influence should naturally be greater because of their heightened involvement. Community currencies can make this possible. By issuing these tokens, DAOs can assign voting power dynamically. It's not just about participation but also about the quality and quantity of contributions. More effort? More voting power. This lends much-needed flexibility to the governance process, tailoring the influence to mirror one's involvement.

Now let's push the boundaries further. In a basic multisig setup, decisions are typically made in Zoom calls or group chats, and actions, like fund transfers, are executed via multisig approvals. However, these tools bring the entire decision-making process under one umbrella. Here, proposals aren't just about moving funds. They can be comprehensive, encompassing discussions, debates, and voting on varied matters. Be it budget approvals, vendor payments, or even high-level strategic decisions like product road maps—everything gets democratically scrutinized.

In essence, the evolution of DAOs isn't linear. The beauty of a DAO lies in this adaptability—the capacity to mold and scale based on the intricacies of the project it represents. As you dive deeper into the DAO realm, always remember that a DAO offers as much flexibility as your vision can encapsulate.

QUEST 14 (ADVANCED): Create a MolochDAO.

Once you've created a multisig DAO, it's time to take the next step and build a more sophisticated DAO.

Go to daohaus.club and click "summonDAO," which will let you choose the parameters of your new DAO and create it onchain. You can always add other members later.

To avoid paying $100 in gas fees, you should use Polygon or Optimism; just switch the network in the right corner of the screen.

As always, you can find detailed instructions at howtodao.xyz/quest.

When diving deeper into the construction of a DAO, especially with platforms like Moloch, you'll notice options that allow you to select between transferable and nontransferable tokens. This distinction is critical.

While the initial impression might suggest that all tokens have an inherent value, acting as financial instruments, this isn't always the case. Nontransferable tokens introduce a reputation-based system, effectively tying the token to a specific address/individual. Such a system prioritizes collaboration with trusted partners, mitigating the risk of external actors buying out tokens and disrupting the governance system.

Another protection for individual members is introduced by the RAGEQUIT function within MolochDAO, offering participants a trustless exit strategy. Imagine diverging visions within your DAO or disagreements on spending decisions. Instead of being locked in, contributors can invoke a function known as RAGEQUIT, essentially returning their tokens and claiming their proportionate share from the treasury.

To give you an example, let's say a group of individuals each contributes $1,000 to start a new project. Upon reviewing the first proposal, however, you realize that the approach is not aligned with your expectations, and you decide not to pursue the project any further. In such a scenario, you can initiate the RAGEQUIT process and receive your full amount of $1,000 back, allowing the rest of the group to continue with their projects without any disruption. And you get to use the $1,000 for another adventure.

The RAGEQUIT mechanism is a "give me my money back" button. This mechanism not only preserves individual agency but also serves as a safety net in the wake of events like the infamous hack of The DAO.

Another pivotal feature in MolochDAO is the bifurcation of token types: governance tokens and nongovernance tokens. This division facilitates two distinct roles:

1. **FINANCIAL CONTRIBUTORS:** Those who fund the DAO without having a say in its day-to-day decisions. They

believe in the mission but prefer not to be on the "board." In the Moloch contract, we call these people LOOT token holders.

2. **ACTIVE MEMBERS:** Stakeholders who are deeply involved, holding the reins of decision-making and shaping the DAO's trajectory. These are the governance token holders.

Both categories have access to the RAGEQUIT function, ensuring personal agency regardless of their involvement level. Moreover, the community has the authority to move members from a voting role to a purely economic one. This move does not intend to diminish someone's financial stake but maintains the DAO's harmony. If certain participants disrupt the DAO's mission or ethos, the community can collectively decide to limit their voting power, ensuring that the DAO stays on course.

▌ Customizing Your DAO's Governance

In the world of DAOs, protection of your interests is not only about codes and functions. It is equally important to cultivate a harmonious culture and community. Although the decentralized and permissionless nature of many DAOs is admirable, it is crucial to understand that an unchecked, all-inclusive approach can be a double-edged sword. In order to safeguard the collective interest and maintain a coherent culture, difficult decisions may sometimes have to be made, such as excluding disruptive elements.

Gall's Law states that "a complex system that works is invariably found to have evolved from a simple system that worked. A complex system designed from scratch never works and cannot be made to work. You have to start over, beginning with a working simple system." Essentially, it emphasizes the idea that successful complex systems evolve from simpler, functional predecessors rather than being engineered from the outset. Likewise, many DAOs started off as very simple organizations and grew in complexity over time.

Although establishing a DAO with a detailed governance structure might seem like the pinnacle of decentralized organization design, the journey often doesn't end there. Many top-tier DAOs, having started with foundational tools like Moloch V3 or even a basic multisig, find themselves evolving, charting paths unique to their needs. Sometimes, the available tools just don't cut it, especially when a DAO's requirements are niche. That's when custom smart contracts come into play, and the true power of decentralized customization shines.

Let's take voting as an example. The innovation in the Web3 space has birthed various voting systems that DAOs can leverage. You are already familiar with quadratic funding, thanks to Gitcoin. Its counterpart, quadratic voting, offers a similar revolution in decision-making. It introduces a voting system where participants allocate votes to issues not just by preference but by intensity of preference, paying a cost that increases quadratically with the number of votes cast for a particular option. This method seeks to balance the majority's preference with the intensity of the minority's convictions.

To give you a real-world example of how this type of voting has been used even in state legislation, in the spring of 2019 the Democratic Caucus of the Colorado State House of Representatives collaborated with the RadicalxChange Foundation and Democracy Earth Foundation to bring quadratic voting as a tool to prioritize the allocation of the budget for the following year.

The caucus members had many priorities to decide on, but to simplify the example and show how it works, let's say there have been four projects to vote on and each representative is given ten tokens to cast votes.

Representatives can distribute their tokens among the projects they care about. However, the cost of casting multiple votes for a single project increases quadratically:

- 1 vote for a project costs 1 token.
- 2 votes for the same project cost 4 tokens.
- 3 votes for the same project cost 9 tokens.
- (and so on . . .)

These are the hypothetical results:

- Project A receives 75 single votes, costing 75 tokens.
- Project B receives 100 votes, with 50 residents casting 2 votes each, costing 200 tokens.
- Project C receives 40 votes, with 10 residents casting 3 votes each (costing them 90 tokens in total) and 10 residents casting a single vote (costing them 10 tokens)—100 tokens total.

Even though Project A had the highest number of representatives supporting it, Project B had fewer supporters but more intense preferences, making it the winner in a quadratic voting system. This reflects the idea that the "strength" of preference should also play a role in decision-making, not just the number of people in favor.

This voting mechanism resembles a higher-resolution version of democracy than plain majority voting, allowing a better map of constituency preferences to map to outcomes.

This same system can be used out of the box in your DAO. When Gitcoin, together with Snapshot, a voting platform, brought this system onchain, they allowed anyone to use it. And this is the beauty of our ecosystem; most of the things that get developed by one organization get open-sourced and enable anyone to innovate on top of them.

While knowing how to create a DAO is important, ensuring its success and longevity requires more than just setting up its technical infrastructure. Although it is essential to design a robust governance model and build muscle memory of using it, these elements alone are insufficient to ensure a DAO's success. This process resembles an entrepreneur scouting for a prime location to start a new business venture. Securing the office space and creating effective bylaws are crucial, but the business's success depends on more than just its appearance and technology.

Establish Legal Structure

In the artful progression of building your DAO, crafting a solid legal and compliant framework is important to protect, sustain, and legitimize your entity.

The selection of a legal structure is a bespoke process, as intricately unique as the individual threads of your DAO, varying based upon factors such as geographical location, mission, and specific necessities. This legal encasement shields your organization, providing a defensive stronghold against potential risks, enhancing legitimacy, and fostering more fluid interactions with conventional financial entities and institutions.

Legal challenges loom as possible stumbling blocks upon this path, presenting constraints and hurdles that arise from the often-ambiguous, varying international regulations surrounding DAO entities. An imperative aspect of navigating these uncharted territories involves vigilant, continuous monitoring of regulatory landscapes, ensuring that your DAO remains adaptive and resilient amid the fluctuating legal norms.

Particularly, jurisdictions like Wyoming in the United States, Singapore, the Marshall Islands, Switzerland, and the United Arab Emirates emerge as potentially favorable terrains wherein your DAO may find a degree of flexibility and transparency. The varied offerings of these jurisdictions and assistance from platforms like PEERUP and LexDAO could guide you through the oft-turbulent seas of the legal establishment.

As you navigate the legal landscape, it's essential to remember the tax implications that may arise. These implications are a crucial aspect of your overall legal situation and should be carefully considered.

A DAO, rather than being a means to evade taxation, can actually assist in the accurate calculation of and adherence to tax obligations. This is possible because of its immutable blockchain ledger, which transparently records every transaction. Prioritizing tax compliance not only reinforces operational legitimacy but also instills a sense of ethical responsibility within your organization.

Hence, establishing a legal structure intertwines with your DAO's journey, not as a mere requisite checkpoint but as a fundamental anchor, ensuring that your mission not only persists but also flourishes amid the multifaceted, decentralized realms in which it resides. Crafting a solid and sustainable foundation that ensures legal and ethical compliance is more important than simply ticking regulatory boxes.

Engage with specialized legal minds aligned to the nuanced frequencies of internet-native organizations to guide your steps through this complex maze, ensuring that your legal framework not only complies but also synergizes with the decentralized principles that pulsate at the heart of your DAO.

Develop and Validate Your Offering

With your mission steadfastly anchored, a team carefully curated, a business plan brilliantly architected, and your DAO seamlessly orchestrated and incorporated, it's time to focus on your products and services, with your aspirations solidifying into tangible offerings. During this crucial phase, the creation of prototypes serves as the foundation. These prototypes are more than just preliminary versions of your offerings. They act as explorative vessels through which the viability of your solutions can be validated. These initial creations allow you to distill user feedback and refine your offerings, all while ensuring an unwavering alignment with your organizational mission and effectively addressing authentic, worldly needs.

Considerations around sustainability and ethics become paramount at this juncture: the products or services developed should reflect not merely the mission but your DAO's moral and sustainable ethos as well. If the mission seeks to alleviate world hunger, developing a nourishing, enduring, and economically viable meal solution could be one of the avenues explored. Prototyping enables the pragmatic evaluation of its nutritional effectiveness, tastiness, and feasibility, thereby illuminating potential pitfalls and opportunities early on, safeguarding against subsequent exertions of time and resources.

Creating a more advanced prototype or a minimum viable product (MVP) will mark a critical juncture in your journey. You've validated your concept, and now it's all about getting it into the hands of users, expanding user adoption, and striving for impact or revenue, depending on your goals.

Selecting a technology stack is a critical decision that requires careful guidance toward technologies that can facilitate product development and align with the objectives and community expectations of the DAO. While the Web3 ethos promotes open-source approaches, it is not mandatory. You can choose to develop proprietary technology or leverage funding mechanisms similar to Gitcoin to finance your open-source software, which can provide multiple pathways for early product funding without the need for immediate fee imposition.

In the process, you shouldn't just be aiming to rapidly gather a broad user base; rather, like Airbnb's initial journey, you should try to captivate a select few, ensuring that they become passionate advocates of your creation. Your focal point then becomes capturing initial users' invaluable feedback, refining and perfecting your offerings with every subsequent version.

In essence, this phase is instrumental for getting initial customers, luring investors, onboarding additional contributors, and potentially generating revenue if this aligns with your operational plan. It represents your company's promise, showcasing the ability to create value and sculpt products and services that do not merely exist but also thrive in the market.

Scale and Sustain

Once a robustly established product-market fit, solid legal scaffolding, a meticulously organized team, and a refined road map have all been woven into the fabric of your DAO, it's time to make sure that the strategies employed for scaling fortify your organization's long-term viability and value creation. The challenge here is to maintain an unwavering focus on quality, ensuring that the product or service your organization offers consistently meets the highest standards and resonates with the expectations of your user base.

The path ahead is not a straightforward journey but a continuous process of learning, innovation, and improvement. This phase of the journey is the most enduring, for it is where you will refine your product or service, enhance its features, and improve its impact, all while ensuring that it resonates with your user demographic. This is a landscape where you can reimagine the very essence of your product or service to increase its value and impact until your short-term and long-term goals become crystal clear.

Being adaptable is a crucial advantage, and your organizational culture should serve as a solid foundation for the continuous improvement of your product or service. By embracing collaboration and committing to ongoing learning, the DAO structure guarantees that you can be flexible enough to adapt, even to the point of forking or merging into different product lines when necessary.

Within the vast and interconnected Web3 ecosystem, certain DAOs stand out not for their primary projects but for their auxiliary roles, offering invaluable services and infrastructure to other entities. These DAOs are the backbone of Web3 growth, and they can help your DAO grow. Service DAOs provide specialized expertise to projects that need specific skill sets. Think of them as consultants in the Web3 space. A new project might require governance, tokenomics (the study of the economics of the token system), or even business-strategy assistance. Here's where entities like Bankless Consulting offer insight and guidance.

On the more technical side, organizations like Developer DAO and RaidGuild provide coding and audit capabilities, ensuring that projects meet the highest security and efficiency standards. The importance of such DAOs is paramount. They expedite growth by lending their accumulated wisdom and experience, enabling new projects to tap into established knowledge, saving time and potential missteps.

Infrastructure DAOs go a step further, offering tools and platforms upon which new DAOs can be crafted. They eliminate the need for reinventing the wheel by providing ready-made, audited, and tested systems. DAOs like Aragon or DAOHaus simplify the process of DAO creation, furnishing projects with pre-built smart contracts and more. DAOs like Coordinape or Tally provide tools that other DAOs can use. And for those venturing into product-development areas, there are DAOs that provide specialized technologies that you can seamlessly integrate into your project and build on top of them, like wallet connectivity, DeFi capabilities, or even advanced cryptography, the practice of encrypting information for secure communication.

A noteworthy aspect of this ecosystem is its alignment with the open-source philosophy. While some services and infrastructures might come with a price, many are community driven and freely accessible. Tools like the MolochDAO V3 contract, developed by DAOHaus, exemplify this. It's an open-source and available DAO tool kit for any developer to use.

However, the ethos of the community encourages reciprocation. Successful projects that have benefited from these free tools often give back, supporting open-source developers directly or through platforms like Gitcoin. This cyclical model ensures the continual growth and sustenance of the community. By leveraging free resources and contributing back when they succeed, projects ensure that the Web3 ecosystem thrives and remains innovative.

In the expansive landscape of Web3, service and infrastructure DAOs hold a special place. They're pivotal in ensuring that new and existing projects have the necessary resources, expertise, and foundation. Whether it's technical support, business consulting, or infrastructure, these DAOs are essential organizations in the ever-evolving machine of Web3. The blend of free and professional services ensures that every project, regardless of its stage or budget, can find the support it needs, fostering a spirit of collaboration and mutual growth.

CHAPTER SUMMARY:
How to Build a DAO

- Building a DAO can be as simple as a multisig wallet or as nuanced as the structures that arise from tools like Moloch, but regardless of which you choose, it is essential to determine your governing structure.

- Quadratic voting can be a helpful means of creating a democratic dynamic and ethos within your DAO.

- Pay careful attention to determining your legal structure, and consult with experts as necessary.

- Prototyping will help you to build out your product or service offering and allow it to grow into something useful and essential to your community.

- As you scale and sustain your DAO, service and infrastructure DAOs can provide indispensable tools for doing so.

Part Four

The Future of DAOs

14

HOW TO EVOLVE
DECENTRALIZED
ENTITIES

As of early 2024, there were around 19,853 DAOs, involved in everything from decentralized finance and venture funds to social media clubs, charities, and virtual worlds. As we've said before, they're still in their infancy, despite the fact there are so many of them. The Web3 ecosystem is growing, and there's no doubt they're going to play an increasingly important role in the development of Web3 in the years to come. To be successful, though, a DAO must build a strong community committed to its mission and vision. It must encourage its members to be engaged and to collaborate. And that means encouraging (and rewarding) them for contributing their time and expertise toward the DAO's goals. A DAO also needs a clear governance structure that outlines how decisions are made and how members can participate in that decision-making process. This structure should be transparent—meaning that members can see that decisions are made fairly and with the best interests of the DAO in mind. They must have a shared bank account—a treasury—and an effective token model so members can participate and contribute to the DAO's growth. The tokens should be distributed fairly and have a clear value proposition for holders. Finally, a successful DAO should have sustainable funding sources that can support its growth.

Regardless of whether a DAO is two people coordinating around common resources or millions of people coordinating around larger issues such as climate change, what else makes a DAO successful? Because you can coordinate globally, a successful DAO might take advantage of this borderless ability to organize and do business, to solve issues that are beyond the reach of individual countries, states, or governments. A successful DAO could perhaps organize quickly and efficiently to tackle an issue without getting mired in red tape: one of the biggest advantages of DAOs is how fast you can set up a bank account—the treasury—and establish shared ownership of it using a multisig wallet that is owned by multiple people.

And while it's pertinent to look at what makes a successful DAO and to weigh different types of DAO that exist if you're thinking of joining one, it's also important to consider the things in this space that need to change or evolve: those things that will make DAOs better. If we don't look seriously at that, we're never going to create a better, more equitable model.

Protocol DAOs

Many DAOs emerge to govern a decentralized protocol. Gitcoin is governing the Allo Protocol, which underlines the Gitcoin Grants product. Uniswap is governing its decentralized exchange. And Arbitrum or Optimism DAO governs its own blockchain. As you can see, the use case can vary, but the purpose is the same.

The biggest rise of protocol DAOs was during DeFi Summer, in 2020. A storm of innovation and valuation swept through the space, transforming it from a speculative playground into a burgeoning financial ecosystem with tangible products and substantial user engagement. New platforms, ranging from Aave and Compound to

Yearn and Curve, didn't merely emerge; they flourished, introducing the crypto community to unprecedented services like lending, stablecoins, and yield farming through the articulate utility of smart contracts.

The surge in utility and value of smart contracts marked their transition from a fascinating technology to a vital tool that enables complex financial transactions and establishes novel, decentralized financial protocols. Smart contracts are no longer an experimental technology but a crucial facilitator of robust, decentralized financial mechanisms that bring forward a spectrum of financial possibilities beyond merely speculative trading.

The majority of these new protocols are governed by the DAO, which decides what parameters will be set for their new product or what initiative will be funded to enhance the security or reach of the protocol, all through an onchain governance that gets automatically executed when the vote passes. These DAOs were pioneers in the new protocol DAO category, which has since expanded well beyond the DeFi ecosystem.

Decentralizing Successfully

One of the oldest and most important DAOs is MakerDAO, founded by our friend Rune Christensen to issue DAI, the world's first stablecoin on the Ethereum blockchain.

Like a lot of people in this space, Rune stumbled upon Bitcoin in 2011 and was particularly interested in the concept of sovereignty—the idea that individuals have complete control and ownership over their funds through the possession and control of their private keys, without relying on traditional intermediaries. This was not long after the financial crisis of 2008–2009, and Rune thought the concept was liberating: there was a technology that allowed people to fight back against "evil" governments and injustice. He made money then lost money investing in crypto, but he had seen the potential and didn't want to lose sight of that. He wondered what was next—and that's what led him to discovering BitShares.

This was a decentralized blockchain platform designed to facilitate trading of digital assets, including cryptocurrencies; it provided a decentralized exchange where users could trade these assets directly without the need for intermediaries. The term *DAO* hadn't yet become common, but looking back, Rune says BitShares was a DAO in all but name: this was the first time there had been a coherent vision of what a DAO could actually be. BitShares popularized the concept of "stablecoins"—a type of cryptocurrency designed to maintain a stable value by pegging it to a reserve of assets, such as fiat currencies or commodities, reducing volatility—through its decentralized exchange platform. Rune was convinced that BitShares was going to take over the world.

Rune says BitShares ended up trying to do too much and not executing on individual products. "The quality wasn't there," he says. And that led him to discovering Ethereum. "Everyone was building these cool projects on Ethereum when it launched, and each depended on stablecoins for its existence, but none actually built one." And so Rune set about creating one. MakerDAO, built on the Ethereum blockchain, would enable the creation and management of a stablecoin called DAI. It started life as just a forum—"a bunch of ideological people, mostly from the BitShares community," Rune says. "None had any experience starting or running a business, and there was a total lack of coordination. We said unironically at the time, 'The free market will take care of it,' that somehow our idea would become reality.

But nothing happened. We did a lot of amazing research, but there was no execution. We just didn't have a team structure."

It was a DAO in the sense that all decisions were made on consensus, and it launched a token so that it could pay people for research and work. The project ran like that for two years; anyone could join, and if the majority agreed to a particular action, then that was the action the DAO took. But often, consensus couldn't be reached. The process broke down, and the DAO ran out of money. "The free market wasn't taking care of it—clearly," Rune says. "So from there we went in a totally opposite direction, building a centralized structure, forming a legal entity, getting offices, establishing a proper hiring process and leadership team, and then we focused on shipping a product."

The resulting stablecoin, called DAI, was launched at the end of 2017. At first it was backed by Ethereum's native cryptocurrency, Ether, but two years later Rune launched a multi-collateral DAI backed both by crypto and real-world assets. He believes it's the only way you can scale. Once he'd launched what he calls the "final system"— a multilevel DAI—the purpose of the foundation he'd created was done; it had accomplished what it needed to accomplish. Now they had to dissolve the foundation and create a new, decentralized organization to manage the system: "We created rules in the new decentralized organization and developed a way for it to earn on its collateral and pay out to people and take over the work the foundation was doing."

But, he says, there was no real accountability of what this money was being spent on: "And this total lack of structure morphed into a struggle for resources. People were being paid huge sums of money—Maker had probably the biggest budget paid out of any DAO, something like $40m a year, but it was not producing any value. The budget was not predicated on any kind of result; people were getting paid because they had a cool idea, and so it was pouring money into a black hole hoping something would happen, and nothing happened. The bear market saw its income disappear, and it would go bankrupt if things didn't change."

Rune says the problem was that decentralization without structure results in drama and politics. He thinks that this old-school libertarian logic that the free market will take care of it equals everyone just looking out for themselves. And in DAOs this can mean nasty political showdowns to fire a particular person, or quality people leaving because they don't want to be part of a circus show. The ones who end up staying, he says, are those who can navigate the politics really well.

Here's where Rune's story gets really interesting. He realized that DAOs weren't actually working, that the concept was broken precisely because of human nature: "It was built on this belief that libertarians are somehow superior and crypto people smarter. If only libertarians ran the world, everything would magically be better." But, he says, in the real world you can't have a free market without regulating it. If you have total anarchy, you have demagogues. There was no force acting to keep DAOs decentralized—people would always centralize it. That was their incentive: to take control. And then they'd lie and pretend it was still decentralized. The problem, Rune realized, was that a lot of DAOs were effectively "companies with crypto and a whole bunch of theatrics, where everybody knew the centralized team controlled everything."

Rune realized he couldn't even sell his tokens in Maker because he had too many. If he offloaded them, it would weaken the governance, and the organization could even collapse. He was stuck. It was impossible to get out. And so he decided he had to fix it.

He understood that anytime you had humans, you would have

personal conflicts. In a regular company, to solve them, the boss comes in and fires someone. In a DAO, nobody did that; problems would just get escalated or de-escalated. And there was social pressure on one party or another to step down, so whoever's best at playing politics has all the power.

That's the problem he had to solve. If he wasn't able to directly fire people, he could simply try to create compromises. Rune figured out the solution was to create extremely dense documentation. All of the processes and dynamics and politics had to be written down, and if all the relevant information and variables were clearly defined and explicitly stated—all the details, rules, and conditions were clear and unambiguous—it would be possible to achieve a state of equilibrium. Rune knew that the current premise amounted to let's give everyone the option of doing the right thing or get rich, and what happens is nobody chooses to do the right thing. But, he figured, if you create enough rules, you could create a system where *if* you did the right thing, you'd get rich.

"It turned out to be so much more complex than I could possibly imagine," Rune says. "There needed to be very explicit checks and balances and rules and really strong enforcement of those rules. And we needed to create layers of protections: if the rules were broken, this kicks in. Every time someone breaks a rule, there's a penalty."

The latest version of the documentation amounts to 130 pages. Eventually, Rune says, there'll be thousands and thousands of pages. But members of the DAO really need to read only the part that's applicable to them. And he says the only way to accomplish this is through AI: "We'll use it to generate the text so humans don't have to type up all the ways you shouldn't use money for marketing to pay yourself or your nephew. It needs to be spelled out in such insane detail because anything you don't spell out, that's the thing they'll do. So the more examples, the better. If you can have five hundred examples of what not to do, that's way better than fifty."

What's more, Rune believes there are legal problems ahead for anyone who thinks because they've started a DAO they don't have to follow the law: "It took us eight years with Maker to being close to letting the community run it."

Now, Rune plans to replicate what he's done with Maker so that other DAOs can benefit from the laborious work he and his team put in to establish these fail-safe rules. "If you already have a DAO with governance security, you can apply that to another DAO—and you could even charge for that service," he says. "We're splitting Maker into tons of little DAOs—because we've already built the infrastructure."

The story of MakerDAO is a fascinating example of how organizations learn from their mistakes to become better and more resilient, never ceasing to innovate. Puncar briefly served as a delegate at MakerDAO and can confirm that a lot of politics and drama were unfolding. At the end of the day, though, the technology is astounding, and the achievements of the people involved are truly remarkable. Puncar did not agree with the endgame plan Rune described above, mainly because of the risks associated with such a significant transformation project. He recalled his time in the financial-services industry when a large bank embarked on an "Everest project" to do a major transformation, including of its technology, only to find itself back at the beginning after years of effort and hundreds of millions of dollars lost as a result of a failed implementation. But he's optimistic that Maker will be able to sidestep such a situation. Maker is definitely pushing the innovation in the decentralized ecosystem further, and that's for the benefit of all of us involved.

Democratizing Access

Being part of some DAOs, especially when we are talking about a DAO like Nouns DAO, may require a significant amount of capital up front; the current base price for a Nouns NFT is about 19 ETH, or $45,000 USD. However, there have been efforts to make access more democratic, such as Little Nouns. With Little Nouns, you can work with Nouns DAO or even receive funding through the DAO without necessarily owning the Nouns DAO NFT. Nonetheless, the high capital requirements can be a major obstacle for many people. If we want to make cryptocurrency accessible to truly everyone, we must find a better solution.

Our friend, renowned DAO researcher and podcast host Chase Chapman, definitely agrees that some things need to change. Her answer to why DAOs are so important in the internet age makes sense when you consider how much of our lives are spent online today: "For me, what DAOs actually stand for is the ability to have a voice in these digital spaces that we're increasingly spending so much time in." Chase is in her midtwenties and grew up on the internet; she can't remember a time when she hasn't had access to it, and part of what that meant from middle school onward was that the internet was a really vital part of her social life and millions of people like her. If you weren't on Instagram and Facebook, you were missing out on this important part of the modern social fabric. For Chase and a lot of people her age, whether or not they use the internet has never really been a choice.

But she says the problem was that she realized that even if the intent isn't malicious, the people running these platforms she was using were making decisions that weren't necessarily in the best interest of their users. "And so we don't have a say in the spaces that we exist in online," she says. "Think about the local government where you live. I live in New York City, and I get to vote for who runs New York City. That makes a ton of sense. I spend more time on Twitter [since re-branded as X] than I do in any other space outside of my home, which is crazy. And that's true for a lot of people using TikTok and other platforms. But we don't have a say in how they're run."

Chase studied business at the University of Michigan. Everyone wanted to be a consultant or an investment banker so that they could eventually get into private equity. None of that felt meaningful to her. She worked in marketing for a while but had always been intrigued by the fact that the internet had a huge impact on our lives, and when she first heard about crypto, it was in the context of data ownership and sovereignty.

"What excites me about DAOs," she says, "is that they finally represent a vehicle for having a voice in these spaces we spend time in." Chase believes the long-term impact of DAOs will be more levels of democratic governance for everyone involved. Imagine the equivalent of TikTok in the future, but with levels of democratic governance—one in which users are given a voice. "Right now, having a voice in digital spaces is not the norm, and so my goal with DAOs would be that they would. Whatever you think of Elon Musk, he has done a ton of polls on Twitter: do you think Twitter should do X, Y, or Z. And that should be the default."

Chase wants to see a future world in which we should feel weird about not having a voice in these digital spaces—spaces in which you socialize, but also where you work, how you get paid, all of these different things. In a lot of cases, having this voice will make a lot of sense. And if we don't experiment with that and create a future where this is the norm, we're really limiting what's possible in digital spheres, and that will be a detriment to everyone.

DAOs are not without their challenges. There have been scams and security breaches; there are still some legal gray areas surrounding formation and governance. But Chase says that's not all: "Working for a DAO isn't as safe as a regular job." After she graduated, she was able to move back in with her parents in Michigan. Not everyone has that option, one in which there's a safety net and you can explore different ways of working, and maybe not have the security of a regular monthly income. She was able to start a podcast—*On the Other Side*—that explores how Web3 might impact humans in both good and bad ways. The podcast attracted sponsors, and eventually Chase was able to move to New York because she had a steady source of income.

"There's something we need to acknowledge in the crypto space," she says, "which is that the people who can take risks, like only contributing to DAOs, are not the people who could benefit from these things in a lot of cases." In other words, if DAOs have the potential to change the world, to allow people in developing countries to earn the same amount as their contemporaries in America, then we also need to recognize that it's still difficult to take that leap and join a DAO, knowing there's likely going to be little job security.

A compelling example of the existing inequity in the crypto space, Chase notes, involves airdrops. This occurs when a Web3 project distributes its tokens to a broader community as part of decentralization or marketing initiatives. Typically, the target community is determined based on predefined criteria, such as interaction with the project—meaning existing users—or actions like donating to Gitcoin Grants, indicating support for fellow Web3 communities. Moreover, there can be multiple criteria in place.

So if a particular project announces it's going to release a token to users and investors, it usually attracts the attention of people who like to "airdrop farm"—people who will use products only in the hope they'll eventually get that product's token—a token that at some point in the future will potentially increase in value.

"A recent airdrop was around $2,000 to $3,000 worth of tokens," she says. "Now if I'm struggling to pay rent, I'm not going to hold on to these and wait for appreciation—I'm going to sell those immediately. Even if I'm not struggling, I might sell them. I'm not going to hold on to those unless $2,000 or $3,000 is not a significant amount of money to me. Consequently, crypto rewards those willing to take high risks, because those airdrops could be worth $20,000 to $30,000 or become worthless; it can go either way."

Chase says if crypto wants to adopt the narrative that it's democratizing ownership, we need to find ways to minimize the amount of risk involved and give people other opportunities to earn. In the context of DAOs specifically, Chase thinks that the model of paying people retroactively for work will need to change and that in the future it won't be nearly as common as it is today.

Another issue is this: people often make the argument that because you can be anonymous in the world of crypto, you can't experience things like gender discrimination or racial discrimination. Chase says in theory that makes sense, but the problem is that in practice, it's very different: "The reason that being in a marginalized group is a challenge in crypto is not that people are going to say: 'You're a woman so I'm not listening to you,' although I'm sure people have said that. The problem is that if you are a person of color in the United States, for example, the odds that you can do what I did and live at home for a year and not have to think about paying rent and make just a little money yet still get by just fine are very slim. And this is because of the systems that oppress people of color in the United States."

Chase argues that all of the systems that already exist mean that people who belong to these groups can't take risks like other people can. "My biggest frustration is with people who say that in theory anyone can do X, Y, and Z," she says. "Sure, in theory they can, but in practice there are a ton of systems of oppression that already mean taking a year off and contributing to DAOs is actually not super feasible for most people."

The good news is we're still in the very early stages of figuring out how to compensate people, determining when to compensate them, and thinking about how we approve work and scopes of work. There are things that need ironing out. Traditional finance systems have been in place since after World War II and the computerization of the financial system. Bitcoin has been around for ten years; ETH and DAOs have been around for only about five years.

Give the space time.

CHAPTER SUMMARY:
How to Evolve Decentralized Entities

- **ADAPTIVE DAO JOURNEYS:** DAOs showcase a flexible progression, adapting their decentralization levels based on evolving needs and challenges.

- **PRODUCT-CENTRIC SUCCESS:** Despite challenges, a robust product and market position ensure a DAO's longevity and triumph.

- **PERSISTENCE IN DECENTRALIZATION:** Ongoing innovation in the DAO sphere indicates a commitment to refining the model, providing a blueprint for future decentralized entities.

- **DESIGNING FOR INCLUSION:** It's important to make DAOs accessible to people across the financial and socioeconomic spectrum by designing best practices with these goals in mind.

15

HOW TO LEGALLY
PROTECT YOURSELF
IN DAO-LAND

reating a DAO involves more than just technological know-how; it's also stepping into the varied world of business, complete with its inherent risks and responsibilities. In the same way that traditional business owners have consistently protected themselves from dangers by using legal structures like LLCs and C corps, those who establish DAOs must also create protective legal frameworks around their internet-native projects.

Our journey is guided by the knowledge of distinguished experts who focus their work almost solely on the complex interaction between new internet-native entities and legal systems. Notably, Primavera De Filippi provides significant insights not only through her in-depth legal knowledge but also as a coauthor, with Aaron Wright, of *Blockchain and the Law*. This pivotal book explores the complicated relationship between blockchain technology and legal practice. Furthermore, De Filippi leads a research collective, continually producing and sharing vital research exploring the ever-changing legal environments encountered by DAOs.

Our friend Aaron Wright is a professor at Cardozo Law School and cofounder of OpenLaw, a blockchain-based protocol for the creation and execution of legal agreements. In 2021 Aaron helped draft a piece of groundbreaking legislation in Wyoming that gave DAOs certain legal protections and that we could see rolled out across the United

States. Wyoming had already established itself as somewhat of a pioneer in the cryptocurrency space—it was the first state in the nation to grant a charter to a crypto bank—and the bill that Aaron helped usher through meant that DAOs could be officially registered there, allowing them to operate in the state as limited-liability companies and giving them the same rights and legal protections as traditional businesses under state law. It all came about after Aaron began thinking about the DAO concept and, if it took off, how it would interact with the real world. He figured that we would probably need some separate legislation eventually but that a good place to start would be to wrap it in a limited-liability company. An LLC was, he thought, like the jet engine of corporate forms and offered certain protections. He thought this was the best structure for some classes of DAO—particularly ones that engaged in commercial activities or facilitated investing together.

There are caveats and exceptions, but on a very simplified level, wrapping a DAO in an LLC limits your liability to your activities within the DAO; it doesn't put your personal assets at stake. Aaron puts it like this: "All the crypto stuff's amazing, and the vision is amazing, but the law doesn't evaporate just because you sprinkle blockchain technology or, you know, some marketing phrases on top of it."

What struck Aaron was that there was no corporate form for the internet age. He says that throughout history, ever since the corporate form was invented, each technological revolution has birthed a new form: the age of exploration had state-chartered banks like the ones coming out of England and Holland; during the US industrialization era, state-granted corporations replaced chartered ones. During the railroad boom, corporate structure evolved with the introduction of preferred stock, offering fixed dividends and liquidation priority over common stockholders. People like the Rockefellers and other industrialists played around with different corporate forms at that time, such as trusts and the like.

The age of globalization ushered in the LLC. "It matched the commercial activity that people wanted to do in different parts of the economy," Aaron says. "They needed more flexibility; they didn't want the statutory formalities of a corporation, but they wanted the tax benefits and flexibility that an LLC was designed to provide. But now we're in the internet age, and it doesn't have a hierarchical corporate form."

Aaron figured that could prevent problems for a lot of people online wanting to work together and do something productive. Maybe they could do it in the form of an LLC, but there were limitations there, too. It would do for now, he thought, but "we're really walk-crawling-running toward this fully fleshed out vision of what a DAO is. And I think when we look back or when our children look back, it's going to seem obvious that there should be a corporate form for well-intentioned people on the internet to work together."

Aaron says if you have a group of people working together in the United States and most of Europe, the form is assumed to be a partnership of some sort, but he says there are some parts of how that's constructed that don't seem to work well with groups online: "One example is that in a partnership each partner owes one another fiduciary duty—a fancy legal word for a heightened obligation. You're obligated not to take certain actions that would impair their rights. Well, the notion that an online group operating at arm's length has somehow created a fiduciary relationship I think is a bit attenuated, and, I think, long term, people will recognize that you need a structure that has implied fiduciary duties as part of it. And that is what we did in the Wyoming legislation."

Aaron was the lead author of the Wyoming Limited Liability

Company Act for Digital Assets, which created a new type of LLC that is specifically designed for crypto businesses. People involved in commercial activity, he says, want to be liable for that commercial activity only. That's why LLCs were created. If you have assets, you shouldn't put all those assets at risk—only those related to the business.

Aaron says the LLC met the world where it was at the time—and LLCs have taken over, at least in the United States. The same thing, he believes, will happen with DAOs. There'll be multitudes of different use cases just like there are multitudes of different projects and nonprofits and businesses today. DAOs have the ability to manage very large projects. Aaron thinks one day we'll see organizations with millions of people involved in them in different ways, and they're going to need a method of organization and governance to manage their affairs: "You can imagine organizations struggling if there were millions of people that were part of it. How do you manage that mess? It's a challenging question. But DAOs can do that theoretically."

Aaron's coauthor, Primavera De Filippi, has a slightly different take. She says the problem is that even in these few jurisdictions allowing for DAOs to be incorporated as legal persons, there are actually two separate legal entities at play: "You're actually dealing with one general partnership, which is the DAO, and then one legal entity, which is the LLC. So if the general partnership does something wrong or if the legal entity says the DAO should do something but then the DAO refuses, there's literally no linkage between them." Primavera calls this a "legal fiction." She believes the legal system needs to accommodate the properties of a DAO by actually recognizing the DAO itself as a legal entity, provided that it meets specific criteria. It's an opportunity, she thinks, to expand the scope of legal entities to specific types of DAOs. This is different from what we're doing at the moment, which is simply trying to fit DAOs into an existing corporate form, such as an LLC. "Even if the LLC were to be held responsible for what the DAO does, the DAO could still do whatever it wants," she says.

Of course, there are benefits of wrapping a DAO in an LLC, as we've discussed: you can get paid, pay taxes easier, apply for bank loans, get health insurance. But, Primavera says, at the moment it's the only solution, and an inadequate one at that: "You need a legal entity to be able to enter into a legal relationship with other legal entities. So it's not about being easier; it's that if you don't have it, you can't do it."

The problem, Primavera says, comes when a DAO that operates exclusively as a technical entity wants to interface with a legal entity: "There is no API, or software that enables two or more computer programs to communicate with each other, between those two things because the legal system does not see the DAO unless it incorporates as a legal entity."

Finding a unique corporate form to accommodate DAOs is worthwhile, Primavera says, because of the promise that DAOs hold. The goal is to create self-determining systems that cannot be shut down or controlled by any government, ensuring their autonomy and resilience. Although centralized systems may be easier to manage—at the moment—they also present a single point of failure, whereas DAOs enhance coordination with a new degree of sovereignty previously unavailable in human organizations.

Indeed, as highlighted earlier, Aaron has actively collaborated with Wyoming to pioneer new legislations specifically designed for DAOs. These legislations notably address a pivotal point raised by Primavera: the imperative to not operate one entity onchain and another off-chain without symbiotic interaction. The essence of the Wyoming entity promise resides in the fact that a smart contract assumes the governance role, seamlessly blending both onchain and off-chain entities. Thus, we're not observing two entities functioning in tandem but witnessing a smart contract that governs the entirety of the DAO, inclusive of its LLC wrapper. Moreover, with various jurisdictions progressively adopting new regulations for DAOs, the landscape is perpetually evolving. There are several that have notably assimilated learnings from the internet-native ecosystem, providing opportunities to offer the protective and flexible frameworks that you, as a creator or participant, might need in your journey.

CHAPTER SUMMARY:
Legalities in DAOs

- **NAVIGATING DAO AUTONOMY AND LAWS:** Balancing DAOs' decentralized essence with adherence to regulations ensures participant protection.

- **INNOVATING DAO LEGAL STRUCTURES:** Emerging legal innovations, like Wyoming's DAO laws, enable harmonious onchain and off-chain operations.

- **USING LLCS:** Wrapping a DAO in an LLC limits your liability to your activities within the DAO, protecting your personal assets, and LLCs are increasingly being expanded to cover crypto businesses.

- **LEGISLATION'S EVOLVING ROLE:** Though often lagging behind tech, legislation evolves to fortify and anchor innovation.

16

HOW TO EXPLORE
THE FRONTIER
OF DAOs

The twinkling landscapes of science fiction have often portrayed a vision of an interconnected universe in which different realities interweave seamlessly in the cloud. This might seem like a fantastical future, but in many ways it's already dawning on us. The advent of DAOs and their proliferation into the digital sphere suggest a future that's not just vivid but tangible as well.

Virtual Worlds and Gaming DAOs

The virtual worlds of Sandbox, Decentraland, and similar platforms provide a glimpse of what the future holds. These platforms have created spaces that surpass physical limitations, galleries that transcend walls, and games that are more than just entertainment. They are laying the foundation for a new digital civilization. Facebook's rebrand to Meta is not just a name change; it also signifies a vision of what is to come.

There are projections that the virtual economy, or metaverse, will reach a value of $3 trillion in the next decade. This presents a fantastic opportunity, but we don't want another big player like Facebook to dominate the market. We want ordinary people to contribute and benefit from this economy, and that's why we are creating DAOs.

What makes DAOs transformative isn't just their capacity to foster a digital realm but also their ability to redefine ownership and coordination. With the right planning and governing principles, we can create a future free from the constraints of centralized control.

QUEST 15: Explore the virtual world.

To understand the virtual world that DAOs are helping to enable, it's essential to become a part of it yourself. Go to decentraland.org, click on "jump in via browser," and follow the prompts. Here you can visit a gallery, chat with other people, or go shopping.

As always, you can find detailed instructions at howtodao.xyz/quest.

Beyond the Virtual World

The increase in the prevalence of AI raises the need to consider how it intersects with DAOs. Rather than being adversaries, blockchain and AI can work together. Blockchain can ensure that AI remains a tool and does not become a tyrant. The indelible ledger of blockchain validates transactions, which helps distinguish between human and machine activity. And we have many tools that can do just that; an example of this "Sybil protection tool" is the Gitcoin Passport, which helps distinguish between robots and humans online with impressive accuracy.

MakerDAO is using AI to build intricate governance frameworks that would be too complex for humans to devise. Maker's goal is to document every rule, resulting in thousands of pages, and then verify that these rules are being followed. This process is beyond human capabilities. The automation of such processes could lead to a future where coordination can be as precise as desired.

The future of DAOs extends far beyond AI and virtual worlds. At its core, the DAO revolution promises a world without national borders and economic disparities. As virtual environments continue to expand, so too does the potential for the fair distribution of resources. While there are still challenges to overcome, considering that such a significant portion of the global population is offline, the overall trajectory is encouraging.

One example of this is South America's and Africa's entrepreneurial landscape, where micro-lending initiatives are fostering grassroots innovations. The ripple effect of one entrepreneur's success propelling another's demonstrates that even small steps can lead to transformative change.

Griff Green, the former community manager of The DAO, believes that DAOs could even create a free market for many of the goods and services that we usually expect governments to provide, meaning that they could solve the same problems governments have been trying to solve.

"DAOs can actually create their own new economies that are like central bank economies," Griff says. "They're not getting revenue or making a profit. They're just printing money and giving it to people who are creating value and then ensuring demand for the money. I think we can use the same model to help the homeless. I think we can use the same model to take care of the environment. I think we can use the same model to build roads. DAOs can provide a democratic way of managing the economy."

In this way, Griff thinks that these economies run by DAOs could replace the work of governments. In fact, he believes governments will be their biggest investors: "Let's imagine we had a DAO that issued a currency called Road Coin. Now they also have a reputation token where everyone in the town who owns a house can get one, and they can all vote on things like how and when a pothole needs to be fixed. They begin fixing roads in this small town from a pot of money, and then they make a deal with the city council: they say, how about instead of just burning money by just building roads, how about you buy our token with that money—an investable token. Don't burn the money by just building roads. Buy our token, and we'll build the roads for you."

Griff's idea has been tried before. It's called "community currency": a form of currency issued by private entities or organizations for use at local businesses. The goal of these community currencies is to keep money circulating within local communities and establish economic bonds among individuals in those communities. Very often, these community currencies are issued in places that are underbanked or do not have access to national currencies. One example of a successful community currency is BerkShares, in which USD can be exchanged for BerkShares at banks across the Berkshires, a region comprising various towns and villages in rural Massachusetts. Businesses can accept BerkShares and then use them to purchase services or goods from other firms, pay employees, or support local charitable causes. BerkShares is an example of a successful community currency.

For every success story, there are also failures. Most community currencies fail because they don't achieve a critical mass of people or businesses willing to accept them. But Griff says that Road Coin would solve some of these problems because it could take off in one city, and then the city down the street may want some of that road building action, too. Therefore, imagine that city council buys into the DAO, and as a result the price of the token starts to go up. "Then other city governments begin investing," Griff explains. "Someone sees the model and copies it, and they start a competing DAO to fix roads, and soon there are multiple organizations—multiple micro-governments, you could say—that are managing economies that have created a win-win system around making the roads better. People who care can invest in a start-up that's fixing roads and actually make money off of their investment."

Griff points out that technically you don't need cryptocurrency for any of this. You can build these economies with dollars—and local currencies have existed way before cryptocurrency—but it's too easy to shut down without crypto; crypto makes it resilient, trustworthy, and transparent by default. At the moment, Griff compares DAOs with cars when Henry Ford was making them in the early twentieth century: "When Ford was making cars, cars sucked. Now cars have crumple zones and are run by computers, and they're electric."

Griff wants to see a world in which we use DAOs to reward the people who are creating value for society fairly, and actually make it competitive and efficient to the point where we can build things better than governments can. He says that when governments fail to provide value to society, people start nonprofits, but that those nonprofits are completely exploited because altruists always get exploited by society. "I don't know when the day will come—maybe it's forty or fifty years from now," Griff says, "but there will come a day when there's a revolution in a country and they don't replace their government with another government. They will replace them with a set of DAOs."

It makes sense that DAOs can create better and more localized incentives to ensure that people care about what's happening in their neighborhoods, their cities, and their countries. They can get better involved in the investment decisions and not just follow what their state council gives grants for. Creating local microeconomics has great potential, especially when crypto is global, so what is working in one community can be copied and implemented in other communities. DAOs may not replace national governments anytime soon, but on the local level we can see this happening in the near future. And it can start with something as simple as pooling resources and investing in the look of a neighborhood or organizing town events.

The path to this integrated, equitable digital future may be uncertain, but every monumental shift begins with a single step. As DAOs become more prevalent in our lives, the world as we know it is poised for a transformation.

CHAPTER SUMMARY:

How to Explore the Frontier of DAOs

- Virtual worlds are providing a glimpse into the future, and their significance seems primed to explode over the coming years. In order to prevent these worlds from becoming centralized (à la social media), though, DAOs will be essential.

- DAOs could also open the door to a world without borders and one that doesn't have to rely on governments to make decisions or create infrastructure.

- One possible example of how these infrastructure initiatives could work is currencies devoted to commonly held services or systems, giving stakeholders the ability to weigh in on these features of their lives.

- These steps work best when they happen incrementally, beginning on the local level and ultimately scaling up to larger frameworks.

17

HOW DAOs COULD RESHAPE THE WORLD

t's one thing to talk about all of the changes that DAOs could help create in the world. It's another to picture what that might actually look like. This chapter will explore a few concrete examples, both in terms of projects that have already begun and those that have yet to come to fruition, in order to more fully illustrate just how significantly DAOs could reshape the way we live.

Network State DAOs

The idea of the "network state"—that we could use the technology behind DAOs to start new cities or even new countries—was the brainchild of angel investor Balaji Srinivasan. In the summer of 2022, Balaji published *The Network State: How to Start a New Country,* a book encapsulating ideas that he had been developing for nearly a decade. He proposed that like-minded individuals across the world could come together to form new societies by first building online communities and then eventually transitioning into the physical world, though not necessarily in a single location. He described it as "cloud first, land last—but not land never." In other words, it would begin with an online community, which would then manifest itself in the physical realm. The economies of these prospective countries would be powered by cryptocurrencies, which are borderless by nature. Once prospective citizens established trust and familiarity with one another, they could crowdfund in order to build apartments, houses, or even entire towns where they could live together. These dispersed communities would be connected through a "network archipelago" facilitated by "mixed reality," a combination of virtual reality, augmented reality, and face-to-face interactions. Digital IDs would confer citizenship on each member, and a form of government would be conducted onchain, leveraging blockchain technology.

Unlike traditional nation-states, which are based on geographical boundaries, network states focus on attracting individuals to join online networks based on shared values, consciousness, and moral innovation. These would include virtual universities, an internet-native economy, consensual government with social smart contracts, and integrated cryptocurrency. So where would these new countries exist? The world is already carved up. Surely there's nowhere left to "own"? Ultimately, Balaji insisted, once members of the network state had crowdfunded in order to purchase land, they could seek diplomatic recognition from traditional governments. Then the network state could be governed through the internet.

If this all sounds far too fantastical, almost like science fiction, then you should know that there are already such projects in existence.

Liberland, for instance, is an intriguing case study. Located between Croatia and Serbia, this territory remained unclaimed after the dissolution of Yugoslavia. Vit Jedlička, along with several collaborators, viewed this as a prime opportunity to establish a new state. As they delved into the intricacies of nation building and international recognition, they discerned that a transition to a DAO model could bolster their endeavors. By integrating into the global financial system and adopting a decentralized governance, they believed they could strengthen their nation's position. Rooted in a "live and let live" philosophy, this decentralized structure aims to grant its citizens a more direct say in shaping the nation's future.

Praxis is taking a different approach: it's an attempt to build an autonomous city from scratch somewhere on the Mediterranean coast, a community of members who will live in a decentralized crypto-based city with shared spiritual principles, such as physical health. The city is being planned entirely in the cloud, with Praxis members volunteering to assist in its development, and it is recruiting members from cities like New York, Los Angeles, San Francisco, and Miami. In 2021 Balaji was one of the investors in a $4.2 million seed round. The following year Praxis secured $15 million in Series A Funding.

One of the most adventurous experiments in network-state building, however, is Zuzalu, which is taking a different approach to striking the balance between virtual and in-person existence.

Zuzalu

Between March and May 2023, a few hundred people from around the globe descended on Montenegro, in the Balkans of southeastern Europe. They were there to experience Zuzalu, a pop-up city of crypto enthusiasts who shared a common vision of learning, creativity, sustainable living, and wellness.

In an essay for *Palladium* magazine, Vitalik Buterin explained the thinking behind Zuzalu: "What if cultures or tribes that have formed online with their own goals and values could materialize offline, and new physical places could grow due to intention rather than random chance?" This answer took the form of an extension of traditional tech concepts, but taken to a new level that only Web3 can facilitate.

"We already have hacker houses, and hacker houses can last for months or even years, but they usually only fit around ten or twenty people," Buterin wrote. "We already have conferences, and conferences fit thousands of people, but each conference only lasts a week. That is enough time to have serendipitous meetings, but not enough to have connections with true depth. So let's take one step in both directions: create a pop-up mini-city that houses two hundred people, and lasts for two whole months."

Zuzalu was—and is—an attempt to create a self-sustaining community, where participants immersed themselves in topics like synthetic biology, technology, public goods, privacy technology, health, and longevity. It was an opportunity to come together to share knowledge and exchange ideas, to discover the latest advances in aging research and clinical trials for innovative medicine. At its heart, Zuzalu was an experiment for like-minded people to design and build the city of their dreams. They had come together in the virtual world, and now they were actually together, imagining what a real place built on their shared values could look like. Could they live there together? Could they build infrastructure together? Could they run it like a DAO would be run?

One of the people helping make Zuzalu a reality was Janine Leger. Janine says Zuzalu's creators wanted to take a decentralized approach to how it ran and to build some tech to make that happen. Two hundred people from all over the world—a combination of invitees and some who applied—came together for two months in very close proximity in this small town in Montenegro. "The idea was to bring together people from different frontier tech industries that really wanted to push forward whatever they were working on to collaborate and spend time together," Janine says.

There was a schedule—just like any conference—but what Janine says was unique about Zuzalu was that any attendee could add an event to it and book a space. "That's not normal for any conference," she explains. "Conferences are booked ahead of time; they're built by a central group of organizers. But in ours every event was organized by the community, and anyone from the community could organize something. This meant more interesting, more niche events happening as a result."

Janine says the result was that 100 percent of attendees wanted to see another Zuzalu, which would function as a regular and substantial in-person extension on the work being done virtually. And 90 percent of attendees said they felt happier and more inspired to make a positive impact on the world after the event. At first she said there were a number of people questioning how on Earth they would get anything done. Wasn't Zuzalu one big party by the sea? But, she says, it was clear from the start that status was not associated with who was the best partier or who drank the most shots or who wore the coolest clothes: "Instead it was associated with who was being kind and curious and doing innovative stuff for the world. We had hackathons pretty much every week, and there was an honesty in the status associated with building positive things for the world. So there was this inherent sense of wanting to build and wanting to give back."

Janine says those who took advantage of it from a building standpoint got a ton out of it and were able to build products and have two hundred attendees be totally forgiving about the tech not being perfect. "We were testing it out, and everyone was willing to test it out," she continues. "So as a result, there was more progress. It felt more like summer camp, where as a kid you are still learning a ton. It was an experiment. And it was a very successful experiment where people had a lot of fun. There was a lot of stuff built and a lot of value created. People were a lot happier and felt, across the board, like their minds were expanded. They learned new things, built new things, and I think ultimately we want to figure out how we can run more of these. I want to make sure we learn from DAOs—like being decentralized, and building something where a community can self-organize."

The Zuzalu experiment was a beautiful example of how communities can self-organize. The Zuzalu community built several pieces of infrastructure. Those resources included an Open Source Playbook for building a pop-up city, a privacy-preserving passport to track contributions made by each individual, and infrastructure for funding the Zuzalu ecosystems, public goods, and services. Each of these pieces of infrastructure is internet native and will grow and scale with the Zuzalu community.

As we transition to a more internet-native world, entities like Zuzalu, Liberland, and Praxis represent a significant shift, bridging digital and local coordination methods. With the network state, these worlds will converge seamlessly. Balaji is a really prominent thinker in this space—and the idea here is that we're looking at different scales of coordination: from the person, to the family, to the local community, to the city, town, village, state, country, continent, and even planet. So how do we build a coordination mechanism from a couple of people all the way up to the planetary level? Arguably, DAOs hold the answer. They are borderless, they live on the internet-native layer, they can scale up and down, and best practices can be shared between them. With this concept, we can achieve anything humans can do when they work together. We have our internet-native coordination mechanisms, our digital spaces where we can exchange information but also value, trust, and ownership through cryptocurrencies. We meet on Twitter, in Discord, or on Reddit. And as we move to a more internet-native world, maybe that's what's so profound about Zuzalu, Liberland, and Praxis—this arbitrage between the way we coordinate digitally and the way we coordinate locally. With the network state, these two worlds will meld.

HOW TO NOT FUCK IT ALL UP

Chase Chapman thinks one way to fuck it all up is this sense that there's something about the network-state idea that reeks of colonialism. And we need to address this. Just like DAOs, we need to face constructive criticism head-on; otherwise, how can we respond? Network states are a fascinating concept—essentially using DAOs to run countries or cities or real-world communities. But Chase says that to move forward with them and act like we don't have a history of colonizing places and destroying lives in the process would be nonsensical.

Chase says in theory that network states are a much better system because you're reclaiming a space. But once you get into the power structures like who's in charge, the hierarchy, and who has benefited historically, and actual physical land, you start to have to ask those tough questions because if you're creating spaces within areas where people have been disenfranchised in the past, this is more than problematic. Historical context matters a lot. You've got to be careful that these network states, as Chase says, aren't "white dudes with a bunch of money saying, let's go create our own little settlement."

And Chase is right. We need to be very careful. We need to be aware of the geopolitical history of a place, careful not to take from locals to give to those more powerful or, worse, destabilize countries by splitting them into network states so other countries can keep their power.

On the other hand, maybe network states will be beyond land: that people of a network state would live all over the world but that they would kind of have dual citizenship, living physically in one country but psychologically in a new, internet-native network state. This concept was suggested by our dear friend Primavera De Filippi, a director of research at the National Center of Scientific Research in Paris and a faculty member of the Berkman Klein Center for Internet and Society at Harvard University. She calls it CoordiNations—digital-only sovereign nations. And Primavera says if these DAOs succeed, they need to be recognized on the international level as blockchain-only organizations.

Now, being recognized as sovereign and enforcing that sovereignty is no easy task, particularly if you don't have any territory. Some say it's impossible, that if you live in someone else's house you need to play by their rules. One option is to live outside that house, in unclaimed territory such as Mars or the Moon. Elon's already working on that. But there's still one place you can kind of do whatever you want: international waters. There are vast areas of the ocean that are unclaimed territory. And we could build new countries there.

The other thing we should beware of, Chase says, is that network states might not end up being democratically governed at all, despite them being DAOs. Democracies are based on the concept of consent of the governed—the fundamental principle of democratic governance, which states that the legitimacy and authority of a government is derived from the consent of the people it governs. Network states may be democratic, but they could also be vulnerable to people who emerge as prophet-like figures. It could be hard to avoid, despite a seemingly democratic way of voting on issues and governance. You can vote on issues, but that doesn't prevent leaders from emerging.

"Balaji has this idea of the 'one commandment' in the network state, which is the one thing that a network state centers around," Chase says. "But that is how you end up with cults, where it's this one thing that is of the utmost importance and we're moving our lives for it."

Afropolitan

There is one network state that already exists that's worth looking at in closer detail: Afropolitan. It also addresses Chase's concerns about colonialism insofar as it's not being built by someone from the Global North. Eche Emole imagines a nation-state that embodies the cultural, social, and political aspirations of the African diaspora, one that transcends traditional geographical boundaries and that contains within it a sense of Pan-African identity that is shaped by the experiences, values, and contributions of its members in the African diaspora. And Eche wants Afropolitan to exist in the real world as well as the virtual.

Eche says the best way to understand Afropolitan is to ask yourself, "What does the internet enable us to be able to do today that was not possible in the past?" We've been able to create new companies on the internet—think Facebook, Google, YouTube, and others. We've also been able to create new legal tender on the internet—think Bitcoin, ETH, and other cryptocurrencies. And now we're wondering: can we create a new country on the internet? So instead of a nation-state with land first, this is a network state with an online-first community and land second.

Eche studied political science before he went off to law school. But it was while he was immersed in his studies that he began thinking about the concept of Afropolitan. He drew inspiration from Alexander Hamilton and the Federalist Papers—in which Hamilton asked whether it was possible for societies to create a new governance or constitution through reflection and choice, or whether they were forever destined to depend on their governance through accident and force.

"And we thought: why is there no modern-day nation-state in Africa, or for Africans, that was actually created by reflection and choice?" Eche says. "They were mostly through accident and force, whether through slavery or colonialism. And it's not worked out very well. For the last sixty or seventy years of nation-state experiments for Africans, it's been zero to nothing but strife. Poverty, weakness, corruption—it's not working for the vast majority of folks. And so we said to ourselves: what would it look like to come together with people who have shared values and purpose in order to create a new digital nation? After which we could reach critical mass, and then build out a network state."

Afropolitan caters to the African diaspora through events such as Afrobeat concerts and cultural festivals. It participated in "The Year of Return" campaign in Ghana in 2019, facilitating approximately one million diaspora members' travel to Ghana on the four-hundredth anniversary of the arrival of the first enslaved Africans in the United States. During the COVID pandemic, Afropolitan created a social app called Clubhouse that was used to support collective action, like funding political protest in Nigeria and raising money for the Ethiopian refugee crisis.

Then Balaji Srinivasan published his treatise in 2022: *The Network State: How to Start a New Country*. And its definition resonated with Eche: a highly aligned online community with a capacity for collective action that was able to crowdfund territory around the world and eventually gain diplomatic recognition from preexisting states.

"I remember reading it and thinking: Does this guy know my life or what?" Eche says. "I thought, damn, I feel like this encapsulates what I've been thinking was needed for Africans globally. Like even when there are opportunities for progress, we keep fighting over old tribes, old religions or whatever, but we need to move forward. I thought: We actually have an opportunity to get out of this situation. And so for the rest of the year we red-pilled our way through all the information, learning, doing research about crypto, NFTs, DAOs, trying to understand the technology. And at 5 a.m. on December 23rd, I found myself pacing the room for an hour. My partner said: Hey, what's going on? And I looked at her and said: I know how I would look at someone who's about to tell you what I'm about to tell you, but just know I'm not crazy."

Eche told her he thought they needed to start a new country. That was the beginning. For the next two months, he started finding backers; people from across the world came on board, listened to what he said, and donated. Soon, Phase One of Afropolitan's seemingly lofty plan to build a network state—and eventually a nation-state—had raised $2.1 million.

He developed a four-phase master plan for Afropolitan. Phase One was to build out the network—the DAO element—and issue passports. Eche began with five hundred passports, a manageable number, he figured, which would go to a core group of supporters. They sold out. Phase Two they called "Government as a Service": "How do we aggregate the utilities within our ecosystem? How do we facilitate payments for goods and services?"

Phase Three they called "The Minimum Viable"—how do they build up the credibility needed to be viewed as a country one day? Eche says last September Afropolitan got recognized by the New York Stock Exchange as the first internet country. "This 200-year-old institution is recognizing what we are trying to do," he says. "Today's the New York Stock Exchange; tomorrow it's the United Nations. So you are laddering up your credibility as you go."

Phase Four of the Afropolitan jigsaw was securing the land, but Eche didn't want Afropolitan to have borders. He wanted to combine two concepts together: one was the embassy model, and the other was Chinatown. "Take, for example, the UK Embassy in the US," he says. "Maybe it's a sovereign territory. Then look at Chinatowns across the States; they have their own post offices, their own malls, their own banks and other services. We want to combine those two things together." What Eche says will result is a kind of sovereign "Afro Town."

"Let's zoom out," he says. "Imagine: You're an Afropolitan citizen. You navigate the world with your Afropolitan passport, you're able to make payments for goods and services using Afropolitan currency, and now you're able to get physical entry into Afro Towns located across the world."

The DAO structure means that Afropolitan can be governed by its members. Everyone will have a vote, using tokens, in a massive experiment of a new, internet-native, transparent democracy. "In addition," Eche says, "we're trying to build something that's going to be 'antifragile.' By that I mean it can't be a thing where if the head gets taken off, this whole movement dies. It has to be a thing that lives as a breathing organism of its own. You take off one head, it grows two heads; you take out two, it grows three—because it's decentralized across the entire world."

Eche says "being Afropolitan" isn't about just living in one country; you could be anywhere in the world. That's why he insists Afropolitan has to be borderless—it's a DAO in the real world. Just like a DAO is decentralized, so too is the physical incarnation of Afropolitan DAO, a decentralized autonomous "country" that Eche wants to see existing in every city in the world.

"By virtue of the fact I was born Nigerian, I have been someone who has suffered by a single point of failure," Eche says, using a computing metaphor to describe a malfunction or fault that causes the whole system to stop working. "I was literally born in the wrong country at the wrong time, and it has limited my opportunities, but I've been lucky enough to have privileges that hundreds of millions of people who were also born in the same place don't have."

But we can't rely on the privileged few having opportunities to change the world for the better using this revolutionary technology. As Eche puts it, that's not a simple strategy: "And so the world that we're pushing for is one in which your relationship to the land or territory you're born in doesn't prevent you from opportunities globally." Right now, he says, we have a situation where you might not even be able to receive payments for the value that you add just by virtue of where you are born. "And that's ridiculous. I can't get access to some of my US bank accounts when I'm in Nigeria because they're blocked. They're literally blocking the entire country. People are being locked out of financial opportunities that can help them build their way out of poverty. I think when you navigate the world from a place of being the ultimate outsider, it gives you a very different perspective on what tools and systems you'd like to build to ensure you're never an outsider ever again."

Eche says he's not prepared to wait for this. It can't happen in fifty years' time. It has to happen now, "within our lifetimes." And with the internet, he says, it can, because the internet can accelerate these ideas.

So what's next? What needs to be done in order to realize Eche's dream of taking Afropolitan DAO to the next step—to create these unique and safe spaces around the world that essentially rebuild the entire idea of countries? "First off," he says, "we need to get diplomatic recognition. So will we start by first lobbying the US or the UK governments? No. You begin by lobbying the smaller countries. Then you get a consensus of maybe ten or fifteen countries that have recognized you as a sovereign state and you work your way up to bigger and bigger countries. So the US or the UK, or any of the bigger countries, could be the last on that list. But every recognized country needs an embassy, right? And we're going to need land that's just bigger than the average embassy."

Eche also anticipates pushback. Are there countries that won't approve of what Afropolitan is doing, what it's trying to achieve? Sure. But he says by ensuring they have allies around the world, allies in different governments, it's going to be easier to persuade those who aren't initially on board with the idea to come on board. "We just met the prime minister of Bermuda, and he's willing to work with us to achieve our goals," Eche says. "All you need is recognition from one country to validate what you're doing, and then you ladder up as you go, and you get more recognition from other countries. That's what we're aiming for."

QUEST 16: Explore network states.

To learn more about network states, check Balaji's website: thenetworkstate.com.

You could also consider joining a network state if you find one that appeals to you!

As always, you can find detailed instructions at howtodao.xyz/quest.

CHAPTER SUMMARY:
How DAOs Will Reshape the World

- **VIRTUAL MEETS PHYSICAL:** Network states blend online and offline elements, leveraging online communities for real-world infrastructure and governance challenges.

- **CRYPTOCURRENCY-DRIVEN ECONOMIES:** These entities rely on borderless cryptocurrencies for their foundational economy, enabling global financial participation.

- **CHALLENGING TRADITIONAL SOVEREIGNTY:** Network states redefine nationhood and governance through decentralized, internet-native models.

- **BUILDING A NEW NATION-STATE:** Afropolitan provides an example of how DAOs might be used to create a new nation-state, one that can help to rectify some of the problems created by traditional social and colonial frameworks.

CONCLUSION

The DAO ecosystem is still young, but the concept of DAOs has evolved significantly since their inception. As of 2024, DAOs have gained renewed attention and are experiencing rapid growth, especially with the rise of DeFi and NFTs. Modern DAOs have become increasingly sophisticated, serving as investment vehicles, collector groups, governance bodies for communities, and much, much more. They manage substantial assets and fund significant projects, with decision-making power distributed among token holders. The governance and operation of these organizations have improved, with lessons learned from past failures contributing to more secure and efficient management structures. The integration of DAOs in DeFi protocols, in particular, showcases how they can provide transparent and democratized financial services, challenging traditional financial structures.

Looking ahead, the future of DAOs appears to hinge on several key factors, including regulation, technological advancement, and mainstream acceptance. There's strong potential for DAOs to revolutionize various industries by enabling truly decentralized, community-driven economic systems and decision-making. However, DAOs might face regulatory challenges as governments work to catch up with fast-evolving crypto spaces. Technologically, continued advancements in smart-contract safety and more robust governance mechanisms are expected. Moreover, as more people become comfortable with block-chain technology, and as influential projects continue to emerge, we may see DAOs gaining more mainstream traction, becoming a standard organizational structure for a wide array of initiatives.

Regardless, the DAO landscape will continue to evolve, and who knows what other new developments might occur that will change the game. Hopefully, this book has made you as excited as we are to follow along and participate in that growth. But studying DAOs is kind of like learning a foreign language: you can read about them for only so long before you need to experience them, ideally alongside others who are just as excited as you are. We sincerely hope you'll join our community at howtodao.xyz, where we will be practicing the evolving art of DAOs together.

As of 2024, Puncar is deeply committed to promoting global health and fitness through WorkoutDAO, inspired by his mother's remarkable recovery from a stroke earlier this year, which was attributed to her exceptional fitness regimen. Despite the road ahead, her resilience assures that she will reclaim her prime, shedding light on the importance of health for everyone. Meanwhile, Kevin is working on the development of Gitcoin 2.0, revolutionizing crowdfunding to empower DAOs in funding their initiatives. As you navigate the dynamic DAO landscape, keep an eye on Gitcoin Grants for potential funding opportunities or to discover innovative projects.

This book, along with the howtodao.xyz network and Gitcoin, exemplifies our commitment to supporting your journey within the DAO ecosystem. Through this community, we can incubate new projects and build a bright future for Web3—together.

Appendix

A HISTORY OF DAOs: A TIME LINE

2008 – Digital currency Bitcoin is invented by the pseudonymous Satoshi Nakamoto. It operates on a permanent, public, decentralized ledger called a blockchain. Some say it's an example of an early DAO.

2013 – BitShares, a blockchain platform designed to provide a range of financial services, is created by computer programmer Dan Larimer. Bitshares, a decentralized organization in which token holders participate in decision-making and that incorporates smart contracts, is considered one of the first real DAOs, at that time called DACs—decentralized autonomous companies—and BitUSD becomes the first trustless cryptocurrency pegged to the US dollar.

   – Vitalik Buterin publishes the Ethereum white paper introducing his decentralized platform, which enables smart contracts and decentralized applications. In it, Buterin describes the conceptual framework of DAOs but stops short of calling them by name.

2014 – MakerDAO is launched by Danish entrepreneur Rune Christensen. Built on the Ethereum blockchain, this DAO will become one of the centerpieces of the whole decentralized finance ecosystem and one of the most successful DAOs.

2016 – The DAO, the first decentralized investment fund, is launched by a group of developers, allowing anyone to seek funding for their projects through smart contracts encoded on the blockchain.

- In June, just two months after The DAO launched, an unknown attacker began siphoning funds from its treasury because of a vulnerability in the smart-contract code. They stole $50 million worth of crypto, sending shock waves across the ecosystem.

- Don and Alex Tapscott publish their bestseller *Blockchain Revolution*, which provides the economic theory behind decentralized autonomous business models. They explain how blockchain reduces transaction costs in the marketplace, enabling new corporate architecture, focusing on what they dubbed distributed autonomous enterprises.

2017 - MakerDAO launches a stablecoin known as Dai, aiming to provide stability and transparency in the volatile world of cryptocurrencies.

2018 - Ameen Soleimani and some developer friends launch MolochDao in order to promote better governance within decentralized communities and fund Ethereum-based projects. Moloch is then subsequently forked by dozens of others who wish to run minimum-viable DAOs.

2021 - Gitcoin, the company Kevin Owocki created as a double-sided marketplace to enable open-source software engineers to find funding, becomes a DAO.

- ConstitutionDAO is formed to purchase an original copy of the US Constitution. It raised $47 million of Ether, and although its bid fell short at Sotheby's auction house, it showed the power of DAOs and how they have the potential to change the way people organize, buy things, build companies, and share resources.

- Nouns DAO, an NFT project, launches on the Ethereum blockchain to fund online avatars. One Noun NFT is generated each day and is auctioned off every twenty-four hours, indefinitely. Nouns DAO helps raise awareness of blockchain technology among the general public.

2022 - Financier Balaji Srinivasan publishes *The Network State: How to Start a New Country*, outlining the idea that we can use the DAO concept to form not just new online communities but also new cities or even new countries in the real world.

KEY TERMS

The language of DAOs shares a lot of the same terminology as crypto. Here are some essential terms that'll help you navigate this new world.

Blockchain

Blockchain is a decentralized ledger of digital transactions, maintained by a network of computers rather than by a single centralized authority. Each transaction is verified by the network and recorded as a block, which is then added to a chain of previous blocks, creating an immutable record of all transactions on the network. This may sound like a simple concept, but it has the potential to revolutionize industries as varied as banking, health care, supply-chain management systems, and even voting by eliminating the need for intermediaries and creating a transparent, secure, and tamperproof system of recordkeeping.

Cryptocurrency

Cryptocurrency is a digital or virtual currency that uses cryptography (the process of converting legible information into an almost uncrackable code) for security and operates independently of any central bank or government. Cryptocurrencies use decentralized technology, typically blockchain, to allow secure and transparent transactions without the need for intermediaries. They often have a fixed supply, which means they cannot be easily inflated like traditional currencies. Bitcoin was the first and most well-known cryptocurrency.

Decentralization

Decentralization refers to the distribution of power or decision-making away from a central authority, instead spreading it across a network of individuals. In a decentralized system, no single entity has complete control over the network. Instead, it's maintained by a community of participants who use software and hardware to validate transactions. Decentralization is one of the key features of blockchain technology because it eliminates the need for an intermediary such as a bank or government to oversee transactions, meaning greater transparency.

Ethereum

Ethereum is a platform based on blockchain that allows developers to create decentralized applications, or "DApps." Launched in 2015, it was conceived by Russian Canadian computer programmer Vitalik Buterin. It's essentially a distributed, peer-to-peer network that allows for the execution of smart contracts—self-executing programs that can automate a wide range of functions and transactions. It also has its own native cryptocurrency, known as Ether, but Ethereum has become a vision for a more open and democratic internet-native world, one in which power is distributed and trust is established through cryptographic proof rather than through the traditional institutions of government and finance.

Governance

Governance refers to the decision-making processes and rules encoded in smart contracts and executed by the network's participants. In a DAO, governance is decentralized, meaning the decision-making power is distributed among members of the organization rather than controlled by a single entity or group. The governance process is often designed to be transparent and open, allowing all members of the network to participate in decision-making, propose changes to the organization's rules and structure, and vote on proposals. DAO governance can be implemented through various mechanisms, such as token-based voting or quadratic voting. The governance system may also include mechanisms for dispute resolution, the allocation of funds, and community management. Effective governance is critical for the success of a DAO because it ensures that the network remains secure and aligned with the interests of its members.

Initial Coin Offering (ICO)

Initial coin offerings (ICOs) are a type of fundraising mechanism in which a company or organization issues a new cryptocurrency to the public in exchange for funds. In an ICO, the company or organization creates a new digital token or coin and then sells it to investors in exchange for cryptocurrency. The tokens can then be used within the company's platform or network, or traded on cryptocurrency exchanges.

Permissionless

We're going to turn to our friend Ameen Soleimani to define this concept. "I love bringing up this example of ancient coordination technology—the Vikings," he says. "In fact, you could watch *Game of Thrones* to get a sense of it: They would do these child hostage exchanges. Let me borrow your son, and you'll borrow my son, and that's our guarantee. It's like their whole lives depended on being able to make these credible commitments to future cooperation by putting their children at stake in these agreements. It's essentially the same thing with DAOs. Let's deposit our children into a multisig wallet, and we both need to work together to get our children out of the multisig. But instead of putting our kids in a multisig, we'll put in ETH. It says, 'I'm willing to put some money at stake to represent some sort of alignment interest.'"

Proposal

A proposal is a request made by a member or group of members of the DAO for a specific action or decision to be taken by the organization. Proposals can range from simple decisions such as designing the DAO's logo to more complex proposals like funding a new project or changing the governance structure of the DAO. Once a proposal is submitted, it is usually reviewed by the DAO's members, who can discuss and vote on it.

Quadratic Funding

Quadratic funding is a type of crowdfunding mechanism that aims to allocate resources in a way that's more democratic and equitable than traditional funding models. In quadratic funding, contributions from multiple donors are combined and then matched by a quadratic formula that gives more weight to smaller—micro—donations. This formula ensures that the matching funds are distributed more evenly among the participants, with a preference for those who receive a large number of small contributions rather than a few large ones. This system helps to incentivize the participation of a broader range of contributors, including those with limited resources, and to promote the funding of projects that have strong community support. Quadratic funding has gained attention in recent years as a way to support public goods, such as open-source software and other nonprofit projects, and to counteract the concentration of funding in the hands of a few large donors or institutions.

Quadratic Voting

One way to make sure no one has too much voting power over another member in a DAO is through quadratic voting. This allows stakeholders to have a say in decision-making based on their preferences: by assigning more voting credits to issues they care about, participants can demonstrate the importance they place on specific proposals or choices. This helps avoid the "tyranny of the majority" and ensures that minority interests are represented.

Retroactive Funding

Retroactive funding refers to a mechanism where contributors to a DAO ecosystem are rewarded after the fact for their work. Instead of pre-funding projects or initiatives, retroactive funding assesses completed work and allocates resources based on the value it has added to the community. This approach aims to incentivize innovation and high-quality contributions by ensuring that those who create significant positive impacts are fairly compensated, encouraging a meritocratic and results-driven environment.

Smart Contract

A smart contract is a self-executing computer program that automatically enforces the terms of an agreement between two or more parties. Smart contracts—essentially a digital incarnation of the traditional legal contract, but with a level of automation—are coded on a blockchain platform, such as Ethereum, and are designed to eliminate the need for intermediaries like banks or lawyers to oversee and enforce. When predetermined conditions are met, such as a specific date or a certain event occurring, the smart contract automatically executes the agreement without the need for any human intervention. Smart contracts can be used to facilitate a wide range of transactions such as payments, voting, supply-chain management, and real estate transactions.

Tokens

In the context of blockchain technology, a token is a digital asset that represents ownership in a particular network or platform. Tokens can provide access to a particular platform or network, represent ownership of an underlying asset, such as a company or property, or could be pegged to a stable asset, such as a fiat currency or a commodity. Tokens are often created through an initial coin offering (ICO) whereby investors buy the tokens in exchange for

APPENDIX | 245

cryptocurrency. Tokens can be stored in digital wallets, traded on cryptocurrency exchanges, and used for a variety of purposes like raising funds, incentivizing users, and creating a vibrant ecosystem around products or services.

Treasury

In the context of DAOs, a treasury refers to a pool of funds that is held and managed by the DAO. It's typically made up of the tokens or cryptocurrencies that the DAO has received from its members or from other sources like fundraising events or investment rounds. The funds in the treasury are used to finance the operation of the DAO, including developing and maintaining its platform, paying salaries to its employees, and funding proposals and projects that have been approved by the DAO's members. The treasury is often managed by a committee that allocates funds through a voting process in which members of the DAO can vote on proposals.

Voting

Members of a DAO cast their votes in order to make decisions on proposals, policies, or other matters related to the organization's governance. Voting typically involves token holders casting their votes using their tokens, and the number of tokens held by a member determines their voting power. For example, if a member holds a hundred tokens and the total number of tokens in the DAO is ten thousand, then that member has a 1 percent voting power. Once the voting period is over, the votes are tallied, and the proposal is either approved or rejected based on the outcome of the vote. In some cases, a minimum number of votes or a certain percentage of votes is required for a proposal to be approved. Voting is an important aspect of DAO governance: it allows members to have a say in the decisions and actions taken by the DAO. It also helps to ensure that decisions are made in a transparent and democratic manner.

Wallet

A wallet is a place to store and manage your cryptocurrency. It's designed to hold digital tokens that are recorded on the blockchain. Think of it as a digital safe-deposit box where your cryptocurrency can be securely stored and accessed. Each crypto wallet is unique, identified by a string of characters known as a public address, and is protected by a private key, which is essentially a secret password that allows you to access and manage your funds. Crypto wallets come in many different forms, from hardware devices that look like USB drives to software applications that can be downloaded onto your computer or mobile device. A multisig wallet requires more than one signature or key to authorize transactions. It is designed to provide an extra layer of security and prevent unauthorized access.

Web2

In the very beginning, websites were boring and bland: just text on a white background with hyperlinks and focused on presenting information. Web2, the second generation of the web, which emerged in the early 2000s, represented a significant shift from those early days. Web pages were suddenly more dynamic and interactive, featuring opportunities for communication, collaboration, and commerce—with Amazon and eBay enabling users to buy and sell goods online. It saw the rise of social media sites like Facebook, Twitter, and LinkedIn, which let users connect and share information. Soon there were interactive web applications like Google Maps.

Web3

Web3 is the next generation of the World Wide Web. It's being built on top of decentralized technologies such as blockchain and IPFS. If Web1 was characterized by static web pages and Web2 by dynamic and interactive web applications, Web3 is a more open, trustless, and decentralized internet. It's made possible by several key technologies, including blockchain, peer-to-peer networking, and smart contracts, which enable the creation of decentralized applications that are transparent, secure, and resistant to censorship. Web3 is also designed to put more control and ownership of data in the hands of users. It has the potential to revolutionize a wide range of industries, from finance and health care to social media and entertainment, and empower individuals, promoting greater innovation and collaboration.

Acknowledgments

We are grateful for the support we received during the creation of this book. Our journey into the world of crypto was made possible thanks to our families, who stood by us through the highs and lows, much like the fluctuations in the price of Bitcoin. We also want to express our gratitude to our early mentors: for Puncar, Pavel Rieger, Jakub Hytka, and Lukas Mikeska from the EY digital innovation team in Prague; for Kevin, Brad Feld, David Cohen, Stan Owocki, Alfred Levitt, Manuel Mattke, and Vikas Reddy.

When we first entered the world of cryptocurrency, we were fortunate enough to learn from experienced individuals. Kevin worked alongside Piper Merriam, Joe Lubin, Mike Kriak, Auryn Macmillan, Griff Green, and dozens of talented people at Consensys. Puncar gained valuable experience while working with the EY blockchain team under the guidance of Paul Brody, Rajat Kapur, and Chen Zur. Later, when he began working with DAOs, he learned a great deal from the Gitcoin DAO operations team, led by Kris Decoot, as well as the Lamma team, led by Shreyas Hariharan, which enabled him to become a recognized delegate at MakerDao, where he worked alongside top experts in the industry with Luca Prosperi.

After we accumulated this experience, we wanted to share it with the world. We knew that would only be possible if we gathered a team of experts to help us create a guide to the world of DAOs. Early on, Justice Conder and Ryan Anderson assisted in putting together the book's outline. We also received great support from Bankless DAO, led by John Church and Frogmonkey. Later on, this effort gained traction when we connected with Noah Schwartzberg from Penguin Random House and Howard Yoon from the agency WME Books. They helped us make this project bigger than we ever hoped and spread the word about DAOs to the masses. With the expert help of Alex Hannaford, Kevin Lincoln, and Octavian in the writing and graphics, we made the book engaging, entertaining, and educational.

We knew that we couldn't develop all the book's content on our own. So we sought the views of top leaders to make it more comprehensive and all-encompassing. Everyone was excited about the book and offered their expertise to help us. We are grateful to all those who contributed, namely Aaron Wright, Alisha.ETH, Ameen Soleimani, Anjali Young, Boris Dyakov, Chase Chapman, Eche Emole, Graham Novak, Griff Green, Isaac Onuwa, Janine Leger, Joshua Opolis, Mona Tiesler, PeterPan, Primavera De Filippi, Rune Christensen, Tracheopteryx, Vincent Weisser, Vit Jedlicka, and Yacob Berhane.

Special thanks to Vitalik Buterin, Brian Armstrong, Balaji Srinivasan, David Hoffman, and Ryan Sean Adams, the Ethereum core developers, and Aya Miyaguchi for their leadership and support of the Web3 ecosystem. Your work truly inspires us.

Additionally, we would like to express our appreciation to our expanding community of early partners and speakers participating in the How to DAO conferences. You have been incredible in promoting the concept of DAOs in various parts of the world, as well as online at howtodao.xyz. Thank you for your support!